From Catching Up to Forging Ahead: China's Policies for Semiconductors

DIETER ERNST

EAST-WEST CENTER
COLLABORATION · EXPERTISE · LEADERSHIP

EAST-WEST CENTER
COLLABORATION · EXPERTISE · LEADERSHIP

The East-West Center promotes better relations and understanding among the people and nations of the United States, Asia, and the Pacific through cooperative study, research, and dialogue. Established by the US Congress in 1960, the Center serves as a resource for information and analysis on critical issues of common concern, bringing people together to exchange views, build expertise, and develop policy options.

The Center's 21-acre Honolulu campus, adjacent to the University of Hawai'i at Mānoa, is located midway between Asia and the US mainland and features research, residential, and international conference facilities. The Center's Washington, DC, office focuses on preparing the United States for an era of growing Asia Pacific prominence.

EastWestCenter.org

For information or to order copies, please contact:
Publications Office
East-West Center
1601 East-West Road
Honolulu, Hawai'i 96848-1601

Tel: 808.944.7145
Fax: 808.944.7376
EWCBooks@EastWestCenter.org
EastWestCenter.org/Publications

ISBN: 978-0-86638-266-3 (print) and 978-0-86638-267-0 (electronic)

© 2015 East-West Center

From Catching Up to Forging Ahead: China's Policies for Semiconductors by Dieter Ernst

A preliminary version of this report appeared as *From Catching Up to Forging Ahead? China's Prospects in Semiconductors*, by Dieter Ernst. East-West Center Working Papers: Innovation and Economic Growth Series, no. 1, November 2014. Honolulu: East-West Center.

Earlier versions of the study *From Catching Up to Forging Ahead: China's Policies for Semiconductors* have been presented at the University of California Institute of Global Conflict and Cooperation (IGCC) conference in San Diego on the Political Economy of China's Technology and Innovation Policies; the University of Chicago/Tsinghua University conference on Industrial Co-Development, at the University of Chicago Beijing Center; the University of Chicago/MIT/ Copenhagen Business School conference on Industrial Co-development with China; the Information Technology and Innovation Foundation (ITIF) conference on China's Indigenous Innovation Policy and the Semiconductor Industry, Washington, DC; the American Association for the Advancement of Science (AAAS) Annual Meeting; the East-West Center/University of Frankfurt China conference in Honolulu; the US Semiconductor Industry Association (SIA), Washington, DC; and the Peterson Institute for International Economics, Washington, DC.

Table of Contents

Acronyms and Technical Terms

2G	second-generation mobile telecommunications technology standards, like Europe's GSM standard
3D-IC	a three-dimensional integrated circuit
3G	third-generation mobile telecommunications technology standards, with three competing global standards, W-CDMA (Europe), CDMA2000 (United States and Korea), and TD-SCDMA (China)
3GPP	the 3rd Generation Partnership Project (3GPP), a standard consortium that combines the world's leading standard development organizations
4G	fourth-generation mobile telecommunications technology standards, such as TD-LTE
ACFTU	All-China Federation of Labor Unions
Android	Google's open-source operating system for smartphones
Apple iOS	a mobile operating system created and developed by Apple Inc. and distributed exclusively for Apple hardware
APT	assembly, packaging, and testing
ARM Holdings plc	a British multinational IC and software design company for mobile processors and chipsets
ASE	Advanced Semiconductor Engineering, Inc., Taiwan, the world's largest provider of independent semiconductor manufacturing services in assembly and testing
Baseband	describes a telecommunication system in which information is carried in digital (and, in some usages, analog) form on a single unmultiplexed signal
CEC	China Electronics Corporation
CEO	chief executive officer
CFIUS	Committee on Foreign Investment in the United States
CGP	China Grand Prosperity Investment
CMOS	complementary metal oxide semiconductor process technology
CNCA	Certification and Accreditation Administration of China
CSIA	China Semiconductor Industry Association
DRAM	dynamic random access memory, the most widely used memory device in computers
EEPROM	Electrically Erasable Programmable Read-Only Memory, a type of non-volatile memory used in computers and other electronic devices to store small amounts of data that must be saved when power is off
EU	European Union
Fab	semiconductor fabrication plant
Fabless	a chip design company without an in-house semiconductor fabrication plant
FDI	foreign direct investment
FinFET	represents a radical shift in semiconductor technology, developed by a team at the University of California at Berkeley led by Chenming Hu, enabling a new structure for the transistor that reduces leakage current
Foundry	a semiconductor fabrication company that provides fabrication services to fabless IC design companies

Foxconn	a Taiwanese company that is the largest global provider of electronics manufacturing services, for instance for Apple iPhones
GDP	gross domestic product
GIN	global innovation network
Global Foundries	Singapore-based leading provider of semiconductor foundry services
GSA	Global Semiconductor Alliance, a nonprofit semiconductor organization that supports the worldwide adoption of the fabless semiconductor business model
HCM	Hua Capital Management Co., Ltd, a Chinese private equity investment fund manager
HiSilicon	a Chinese fabless semiconductor company based in Shenzhen, China, and fully owned by Huawei, China's leading producer of telecommunications equipment and smartphones
HK$	Hong Kong dollar
Huawei	the largest telecommunications equipment manufacturer in the world (having overtaken Ericsson in 2012), based in Shenzhen, China
IC	integrated circuit
ICT	information and communications technology
IEEE	Institute of Electrical and Electronics Engineers
ISSCC	International Solid-State Circuits Conference, the world's leading conference series for presentation of advances in solid-state circuits and systems-on-a-chip
IT	information technology
ITA	Information Technology Agreement
JCET	Jiangsu Changjiang Electronics Technology Co., Ltd
LCD	liquid-crystal display
LED	light-emitting diode
M&A	mergers and acquisitions
MCO	multicomponent semiconductors
MCP	multichip packages
MediaTek	a leading Taiwanese provider of chipsets for lower-cost smartphones produced by Chinese companies
MEMS	microelectromechanical systems
MIIT	Ministry of Industry and Information Technology
MLP	Medium- and Long-Term Plan for Science and Technology Development 2006–2020
MLPS	China's National Information Assurance Policy Framework Multi-Level Protection Scheme that seeks to extend cyber-security regulations well beyond sensitive military and government agencies to cover many nongovernment end users
MoF	Ministry of Finance
Moore's Law	the observation, developed by Gordon Moore, a former CEO of Intel, that, over the history of computing hardware, the number of transistors in a dense integrated circuit has doubled approximately every two years
MOQ	minimum order quantity that chip design companies must meet to qualify for service contract with leading IC foundry service providers
MoST	Ministry of Science and Technology
MPU	microprocessor unit
NDRC	National Development and Reform Commission
nm	nanometers (1 nm = 1.0×10^{-7} centimeters)
OEM	original equipment manufacturer
OS	operating system

PC	personal computer
PV	photovoltaic
R&D	research and development
RDA	RDA Microelectronics, a Chinese IC design company that has been merged with the Chinese IC design company Spreadtrum
RF	radio-frequency electronics
RMB	renminbi (official currency of China)
SASAC	Assets Supervision and Administration Commission of the State Council
SCI	Science Citation Index
SEI	China's Strategic Emerging Industries plan
SEMI	Semiconductor Equipment and Materials International, an industry association
SIA	the US Semiconductor Industry Association
SILG	China State Informatization Leaders Group
SME	small- and medium-sized enterprises
SMIC	Semiconductor Manufacturing International Corporation, China's leading semiconductor foundry
SOE	state-owned enterprise
Spreadtrum	a leading Chinese IC design company
SRAM	static random-access memory is faster and more expensive than DRAM; it is typically used to support processors while DRAM is used for a computer's main memory
S&T	science and technology
TD-LTE	time-division long-term evolution, one of the competing fourth-generation mobile communication standards, submitted by China to the International Telecommunications Union
TD-SCDMA	time-division synchronous code division multiple access, one of three competing third-generation mobile communication standards, submitted by China to the International Telecommunications Union
TI	Texas Instruments
TSMC	Taiwan Semiconductor Manufacturing Co., the world's largest semiconductor foundry
UN	United Nations
UMC	United Microelectronics Corporation, the world's second largest semiconductor foundry
USITO	United States Information Technology Office, an organization that observes and analyzes China's policies in the information and communication industry, including semiconductors
Wafer	a thin slice of semiconductor material, such as a crystalline silicon, used in electronics for the fabrication of integrated circuits
WTO	World Trade Organization
Xiaomi	a Chinese vendor of lower-cost smartphones that tried to forge ahead without developing a broad portfolio of intellectual property rights
ZTE	China's second largest telecommunications equipment vendor

Executive Summary

China has reached a level of development where catching up through an investment-driven development model is no longer sufficient to create long-term economic growth and prosperity. The closer China has moved to the technology frontier, the less scope there is for imitation and low-level incremental innovation. Of critical importance now is that Chinese firms develop and protect their own intellectual property rights and accelerate the commercialization of new ideas, discoveries, and science-based industrial inventions.

Since the Third Plenum, China's leadership has emphasized the need to upgrade the economy through productivity-enhancing industrial innovation. To make this happen, the government has embarked on major changes in China's innovation strategy and its science and technology system. Emblematic of the shift to an innovation-driven development model are new policy initiatives in China's semiconductor industry that seek to accelerate the transition from catching up with global industry leaders to forging ahead through innovation.

The semiconductor industry is one of the priority targets of China's innovation policy. At the same time, China's semiconductor industry is deeply integrated into the global semiconductor industry through markets, investment, and technology. Thus, the industry provides an interesting test case for studying the strengths and weaknesses of China's push toward an innovation-driven development model.

Drawing on interviews with China-based industry experts, this study takes a close look at objectives, strategy, and implementation policies of China's new push in semiconductors, and it examines what this implies for China's prospects in this industry. The following questions are addressed in particular: *In light of the mixed results of earlier support policies in this industry, how realistic are the objectives, outlined in the new semiconductor strategy? Does the semiconductor strategy signal a resurgence of state-led mercantilist industrial policies? In other words, is the government just pouring old wine into new bottles? Or are there signs of real adjustments in strategy and policy implementation as the government seeks to exploit global transformations in markets and technology, and as it seeks to benefit from the rise of private firms in China's semiconductor industry?*

In addressing these questions, the study contributes to the literature three observations: First, top-down, state-led "old industrial policies" simply don't work in a knowledge-intensive and highly globalized industry like semiconductors, where basic parameters that determine how China will fare may change at short notice and in unpredictable ways. Rising complexity of technology, business organization, and competitive dynamics are the root causes for such uncertainty. If China wants to forge ahead in the semiconductor industry, it needs to move toward a bottom-up, market-led approach to industrial policy.

Second, the rise of private firms in China's semiconductor industry further strengthens the argument for a bottom-up and gradually more market-led approach to industrial policy. Over the last 60 or so years, China's semiconductor industry has come a long way from being a completely government-owned part of the defense technology production system, with state-owned enterprises (SOEs) as the only players, toward a gradually more market-led development model. The role of SOEs has dramatically declined, and a deep integration into international trade and global networks of production and innovation has transformed decisions on pricing and investment allocation, with private firms as the main drivers.

Third, while China's progressive integration into the international economy has unshackled market forces in the semiconductor industry, China's policies to develop this industry still carry the burden of the old-style, top-down industrial policy. The result has been an unresolved friction between state and market, where policymakers and planners prescribe desired outcomes (in terms of growth rates, technology, and "indigenous innovation" products), but fail to take into account the need of industry, and in particular private firms, for global technology sourcing.

The study explores whether China's new policy on semiconductors signals at least incremental movements toward a more bottom-up, market-led approach to industrial policy.

Part One demonstrates that China's achievements in semiconductors are overshadowed by persistent weaknesses, despite massive earlier support of the government. China is still playing second fiddle in the industry, because the state's indigenous innovation policy collides with the global technology sourcing needs of Chinese semiconductor firms.

As long as the state shapes the overall strategy from above, state and market will not work together well. This is not primarily because market forces may not be allowed to operate freely. In fact, China's indigenous innovation policy arguably relies more on using incentives (such as subsidies or government procurement), rather than restrictions on inputs, to promote local technologies.

An important weakness of China's indigenous innovation policy lies in its top-down implementation. China's leadership continues to retain control over the selection of priority sectors, technologies, and areas of public development. Industry participants complain that when push comes to shove, vested interests in government agencies tend to override suggestions from industry experts. As long as this top-down approach to industrial policy prevails, China's leadership may end up having only incomplete knowledge of the real and continuously evolving needs of diverse private firms in terms of global knowledge sourcing.

A second weakness of China's indigenous innovation policy is the focus on challenges facing China's transition to innovation-led development, especially with regard to licensing costs and cybersecurity. Those challenges are real and need to be addressed. But in fighting those challenges, China's innovation policy tends to neglect the vast opportunities that result from China's deep integration into the global semiconductor value chain, in terms of learning, the development of innovation capabilities, and the implementation of best-practice management techniques and institutions. This can create an important barrier to innovation, because both domestic and foreign investors expect such policies, and their conduct changes accordingly.

The unresolved friction between state and market poses a fundamental question for the remainder of this study: What changes in policy would be needed to combine the benefits of both innovation strategies—indigenous innovation and global technology sourcing?

Part Two of the study takes a closer look at two policy initiatives to implement China's new semiconductor strategy: (a) the **IC Industry Support Small Leading Group** to enhance strategy coordination; and (b) "market-driven" **IC Industry Equity Investment Funds** to improve investment allocation, and to enhance firm size and capabilities through strategic partnerships, joint ventures, and mergers and acquisitions, involving both foreign firms and domestic firms.

The implementation of both policies signals a genuine effort to experiment with new and hybrid approaches to industrial policy that combines top-down decision making with bottom-up approaches, especially for investment funding and for the organization of technical working groups that provide important insights into strategy formulation. The study shows that the new policy relies on private equity investment rather than subsidy as the primary tool. The government participates in equity investment and claims it will do so without intervening with management decisions. In essence, this policy is expected to reduce the cost of investment funds for a selected group of firms, which is to form a "national team" in the semiconductor industry. With equity ownership, the government believes that it can better monitor the performance of the firms than in the case of subsidy. If the firms do not perform, the government can replace the management teams.

It remains unclear, however, how this approach is different from the case of state-owned enterprises, where the government can also monitor and replace the management. A related unresolved puzzle is how private equity fund managers, who are supposed to maximize the return to capital, can nevertheless serve as proxies for the government and support its policy to strengthen indigenous innovation.

China's new policy to upgrade its semiconductor industry through innovation does not represent a radical break with a deeply embedded statist tradition. Within these boundaries, however, the study detects important changes in the direction of a bottom-up, market-led approach to industrial policy.

Part Three explores the basic economics that shape China's efforts to upgrade its semiconductor industry. China's leadership is very conscious that the United States is far ahead in advanced semiconductors and that China has a long way to go to close this gap. At the same time, however, China's new policies for semiconductors also convey a new sense of optimism. Global transformations in semiconductor markets and technology are no longer only perceived as threats. In fact, China's technology planners now seek to identify pathways to innovation-led development for China's semiconductor industry that could benefit from four global transformations: (a) the demand pull from mobile devices, (b) new opportunities for China's foundries in trailing-node semiconductor technologies, (c) changes in the IC foundry industry landscape, and (d) a new interest in strategic partnerships and mergers and acquisitions (M&A). To exploit the tailwinds from the market, the government is encouraging strategic partnerships and acquisitions, both among domestic firms and with leading global players.

The study examines the economic rationale behind each of these four perceived opportunities and what factors might determine China's chances of success. While the opportunities are real, their precarious nature also involves considerable uncertainty. In other words, basic parameters that determine how China will fare may change at short notice and in unpredictable ways. If China wants to exploit the above opportunities, it needs to move toward a bottom-up, market-led approach to industrial policy, guided by the principle of "smart specialization."

In response to the rising complexity and uncertainty of today's semiconductor industry, the government seems more open to experimentation with new, more market-driven approaches to investment finance and flexible, bottom-up policy implementation, based on multilayered industrial dialogues with private firms. China's policies to forge ahead in semiconductors thus provide an interesting example of China's current efforts to move from investment-driven catching up to an innovation-driven development model.

The findings raise important questions for further research. For instance, as highlighted in Part Three of the study, it is unclear how long China's domestic demand pull for mobile devices, and especially smartphones, can continue to compensate for shrinking foreign markets as an important driver of demand for China's semiconductors. There is reason to ask this question, as demand growth in the Chinese smartphone market has been slowing down since early 2015. In addition, China's semiconductor strategy seems to have largely neglected, thus far, its impact on China's critically important exports of electronic final products. In fact, key policy documents on the development of China's semiconductor industry provide little guidance on this critical issue.

The study concludes with a brief discussion of four factors that could derail China's transition to innovation-led growth in semiconductors: overcapacity, China's fragmented innovation system, the leadership's cybersecurity objectives, and possible impacts of new international trade and investment agreements.

In light of the rising uncertainty that results from China's progressive integration into the global IT industry, the study culminates in a plea that China experiment further with new, more market-driven and flexible approaches to industrial policy. Prioritization is no longer the exclusive role of the state planner. The focus of policymaking needs to shift from the selection of priority sectors, technologies, and areas for public investment to the facilitation of an interactive learning process in which the private sector is discovering and producing information about new activities. The government in this new model of industrial policy provides incentives and removes regulatory constraints for the search to happen, it assesses the potential of those ideas, and it empowers those actors most capable of realizing that potential.

From Catching Up to Forging Ahead: China's Policies for Semiconductors

"It is not just today, when we are scientifically and technically backward, that we need to learn from other countries—after we catch up with advanced-world levels in science and technology, we shall still have to learn from the strong points of others."[1]

Deng Xiaoping, March 28, 1978, on the critical importance of global knowledge sourcing, even once China nears the limits of catching up

"The Chinese people are involved in the great historical task of building up the nation after a century of chaos. Keep this in mind, and much that would be incomprehensible becomes clear and predictable."[2]

Tim Clissold, author of Mr. China: A Memoir[3]

"Pragmatism has been a hallmark of China's reforms over the past thirty years, as Chinese leaders have not flinched from a realistic view of their challenges. They typically experiment with various approaches before deciding on the best ways to address major concerns."[4]

Ken Lieberthal, Brookings Institution

"In the next ten years, there will be a large amount of M&A cases in China, but many of them will fail...But it is better than nothing. China's enterprises will gain experience."[5]

Chen Datong, chairman, Hua Capital Management Co., Ltd, which manages one of China's IC Industry Equity Development Funds

China's Important New Push in Semiconductors

Recent developments in China's semiconductor industry signal an important change in the direction of its development strategy. A seminal study, jointly published in 2012 by the World Bank and the Development Research Center of the State Council of China, argued that reliance on catching up through an investment-driven development model is no longer sufficient to create long-term economic growth and prosperity.[6] Xue Lan, for instance, argues that due to serious constraints on financial, human, and environmental resources, "[e]conomic growth based on scale expansion is running out of steam."[7] And Liu Xielin observes that the closer China has moved to the technology frontier, the less scope there is for imitation and low-level incremental innovation. Of critical importance now is that Chinese firms develop and protect their own intellectual property rights and accelerate the commercialization of new ideas, discoveries, and science-based industrial inventions.[8]

In fact, China's leadership since the Third Plenum has emphasized the need to upgrade the economy through productivity-enhancing industrial innovation.[9] To make this happen, the government has embarked on major changes in China's innovation strategy and in its science and technology system.[10]

Rapid catching up through foreign direct investment (FDI)–based technology imports and imitation was driven by a top-down innovation system with a focus on quantitative indicators, such as increasing R&D intensity, number of Science Citation Index (SCI) publications, reduction of patent licensing fees, and growth of patent applications. State-owned enterprises (SOEs) were supposed to be the main carriers of innovation. In fact, "since 2008, MoST (Ministry of Science and Technology), together with the state-owned Assets Supervision and Administration Commission of the State Council (SASAC) and the All-China Federation of Labor Unions (ACFTU), elected dozens of innovative firms each year. The majority of the firms selected are SOEs in manufacturing industries."[11]

Emblematic of the shift to an innovation-driven development model are new policy initiatives, which are focused, for instance, on the development and protection of intellectual property rights; a move toward effective, efficient, and transparent regulations; the involvement of private investment firms to improve the allocation of funds; a push to reduce the fragmentation of China's innovation system through improved coordination among government agencies and between the central government and local governments; and support for the commercialization of research projects.

Overall, the new strategy emphasizes an expanded role for market forces to determine economic outcomes. However, persistent resistance by powerful vested interests, especially from leading SOEs, gave rise to quite ambiguous formulations of key objectives. Nevertheless, on October 20, 2014, the government announced a major shake-up of China's science and technology (S&T) governance and program structure. A "ministerial joint meeting system" was put in place to manage the changes, chaired by the minister of S&T and supported by China's powerful National Development and Reform Commission (NDRC) and the Ministry of Finance. All S&T programs where projects are selected through a competitive process will be managed by third-party institutes rather than by ministries—such as MoST and MIIT, where they are currently located—and there will be a focus on China's national strategic development projects. Introduction of a transparent and effective peer review system should be accompanied by an increased emphasis on industry needs.[12]

The semiconductor industry is one of the priority targets of China's innovation policy, as codified in the Medium- and Long-Term Plan for Science and Technology Development (MLP) and in the Strategic Emerging Industries (SEI) plan published in 2012.[13] At the same time, China's semiconductor industry is deeply integrated in the global semiconductor industry value chain through markets, investment, and technology.[14] This industry thus provides an interesting test case for studying the strengths and weaknesses of China's push toward an innovation-driven development model. In fact, China's new strategy to upgrade its semiconductor industry (outlined in the **Guidelines to Promote National Integrated Circuit Industry Development**, June 24, 2014[15]) seeks to move from the catching-up stage to a full-scale forging ahead. Plans are to strengthen China's industry simultaneously through advanced manufacturing and innovation capabilities in the integrated circuit (IC) design industry and through domestic IC fabrication, primarily through foundry services.

This study takes a close look at objectives, strategy, and implementation policies of China's new push in semiconductors, and examines what this implies for China's prospects in this industry. The following questions are addressed in particular: *In light of the mixed results of earlier support policies in this industry, how realistic are the objectives, outlined in the* Guidelines? *Does the semiconductor strategy signal a resurgence of state-led mercantilist industrial policies? In other words, is the government just filling old wine into new bottles? Or are there signs of real adjustments in strategy and policy implementation as the government seeks to exploit global transformations in markets and technology, and as it seeks to benefit from the rise of private firms in China's semiconductor industry?*

In addressing these questions, the study contributes to the literature three **observations**: *First*, top-down, state-led "old industrial policies" simply don't work in a knowledge-intensive and highly globalized industry like semiconductors, where basic parameters that determine how China will fare may change at short notice and in unpredictable ways.[16] Rising complexity of technology, business organization, and competitive dynamics are the root causes for such uncertainty.[17] If China wants to forge ahead in the semiconductor industry, it needs to move toward a bottom-up, market-led approach to "industrial policy."

There is ample evidence in the literature that latecomers like China need industrial support policies to catch up and develop a robust industrial ecosystem.[18] But this does not imply old-style, top-down industrial policies. In fact, forging ahead through innovation requires a sophisticated mix of government support policies and market-driven approaches to investment finance, as well as a capacity for flexible policy adjustments based on multilayered industrial dialogues with private firms.

Second, the rise of private firms in China's semiconductor industry further strengthens the argument for a bottom-up and gradually more market-led approach to industrial policy. Over the last 60 or so years, China's semiconductor industry has come a long way, evolving from a completely government-owned part of the defense technology production system, with SOEs as the only players, toward a gradually more market-led development pattern. The role of SOEs has dramatically declined, and a deep integration into international trade and global networks of production and innovation has transformed decisions on pricing and investment allocation, with private firms as the main drivers.[19]

Third, while China's progressive integration into the international economy has unshackled market forces in the semiconductor industry, its policies to develop this industry still carry the legacy burden of the old-style, top-down industrial policy. The result has been an unresolved friction between the state and the market, where policymakers and planners prescribe desired outcomes (in terms of growth rates, technology, and "indigenous innovation" products), but fail to take into account the needs of industry, particularly private firms, for global technology sourcing.

The study explores whether China's new policy on semiconductors signals at least incremental movements toward a more bottom-up, market-led approach to "industrial policy."

Part One demonstrates that China's achievements in semiconductors are overshadowed by persistent weaknesses, despite massive earlier support from the government. It is argued that China is still playing second fiddle in this industry, because the state's "indigenous innovation policy" collides with the "global technology sourcing" needs of Chinese semiconductor firms.

As long as the state shapes the overall strategy from above, the state and the market do not work together well. This is not primarily because market forces are not allowed to operate freely. In fact, China's indigenous innovation policy arguably relies more on using incentives (such as subsidies or government procurement) rather than restrictions on inputs to promote local technologies. For instance, some leading Chinese equipment producers, such as Lenovo and Huawei, are largely free to choose the processors and other core components (domestic or foreign) to be used in their products. In that sense, the government does not restrict their needs for global technology sourcing.

An important weakness of China's indigenous innovation policy lies in its top-down implementation. China's leadership continues to retain control over the selection of priority sectors, technologies, and areas of public development. In the semiconductor industry, the China Semiconductor Industry Association (CSIA) has provided a forum for strategic brainstorming. It also has provided support services to small Chinese IC design firms. But industry participants complain that when push comes to shove, vested interests in government agencies tend to override suggestions from industry experts. Much more needs to be done to establish real, intense, and multilayered industrial dialogues between the diverse stakeholders of this industry.

In any case, before China's new policy on semiconductors was released, it was fair to argue that China's leadership had only incomplete knowledge of the real and continuously evolving needs of diverse private firms in terms of global knowledge sourcing. Contemporary innovation theory emphasizes that innovation results from the interactions of multiple and diverse stakeholders through geographically dispersed innovation networks. To paraphrase Cristiano Antonelli, innovation in China thus requires complex systems that are characterized by the heterogeneity of agents with different functions, different endowments, different learning capabilities, different perspectives, and—most importantly—different locations in the multidimensional spaces of geography, knowledge, technology, and reputation. [20]

A second weakness of China's indigenous innovation policy concerns its focus on the challenges of transitioning to innovation-led development, especially with regard to licensing costs and cybersecurity. These challenges are real and need to be addressed. In wrestling with these challenges, however, innovation policy tends to neglect the vast opportunities that result from China's deep integration into the global semiconductor value chain, in terms of learning, the development of innovation capabilities, and best-practice management techniques and institutions. To respond effectively to perceived challenges, the state sometimes seeks to constrain market forces, in line with China's still deeply entrenched planned economy legacy. This can create an important barrier to innovation, because both domestic and foreign investors expect such interference, and their conduct changes accordingly.[21]

The unresolved friction between state and market poses a fundamental question for the remainder of this study: What changes in policy would be needed to combine the benefits of both innovation strategies—indigenous innovation and global technology sourcing?

Part Two reviews what we know about objectives and strategy that shape China's new push in semiconductors. In the leadership's view, the new strategy needs to address both persistent domestic weaknesses and new opportunities resulting from global transformations in semiconductor markets and technology. Part Two also takes a closer look at two policy initiatives to implement the new strategy: (a) the **IC Industry Support Small Leading Group** to enhance strategy coordination; and (b) "market-driven" **IC Industry Equity Investment Funds** to improve investment allocation, and to enhance firm size and capabilities through strategic partnerships, joint ventures, and mergers and acquisitions, involving both foreign firms and domestic firms.

The implementation of both policies signals a genuine effort to experiment with new and hybrid approaches to industrial policy that combine top-down policy implementation with sometimes still experimental bottom-up approaches, especially for investment funding and for the organization of technical working groups that provide important insights in strategy formulation.

Part Three explores the basic economics that shape China's efforts to upgrade its semiconductor industry. Rising complexity and increasing uncertainty determine the new world of international economics shaped by globalization. A defining characteristic of globalization is the emergence of international corporate networks that integrate dispersed production, engineering, product development, and research across geographic borders. Knowledge-sharing is the glue that keeps these networks growing. The result is an increase in the organizational and geographical mobility of knowledge.

These fundamental transformations of the global economy have been analyzed elsewhere in detail.[22] The focus of this study is on global transformations in semiconductor markets and technology, which provide a demand pull from mobile devices for domestic IC design companies, and upgrading opportunities for China's IC foundries in trailing-node integrated circuit process technologies (28 nanometers and above). To exploit the tailwinds from the market, the government is encouraging strategic partnerships and acquisitions, both among domestic firms and with leading global players. The study shows that, in response to the rising complexity and uncertainty of today's semiconductor industry, the government seems more open to experimentation with new, more market-driven approaches to investment finance and flexible, bottom-up policy implementation, based on multilayered industrial dialogues with private firms. China's policies to forge ahead in semiconductors thus provide an interesting example of current efforts to move from investment-driven catching up to an innovation-driven development model.

However, China's semiconductor strategy seems to have largely neglected, thus far, its impact on the critically important exports of electronic final products. In fact, key policy documents on the development of China's semiconductor industry provide little guidance on this critical issue. This checkered experience in China's semiconductor industry supports Liu Xielin's proposition that the transition to an innovation-led development model is likely to occur gradually rather than in a big "leap-frogging" push.[23] Given the size of the country and its enormous unresolved problems, it is hardly surprising that the transition in semiconductors is messy and full of contradictions.

The findings of this study raise important questions for further research. For instance, as highlighted in Part Three of the study, it is unclear how long China's semiconductor industry can rely on the domestic demand pull for mobile devices, and especially smartphones. In fact, demand growth in the Chinese smartphone market has been slowing down since early 2015. It is thus quite uncertain whether and how long China's demand pull for mobile devices can compensate for shrinking demand in foreign markets.

The study concludes with a brief discussion of four factors that could derail China's transition to innovation-led growth in semiconductors: over-capacity, a fragmented innovation system, the leadership's cybersecurity objectives, and possible impacts of new international trade and investment agreements. In light of the rising uncertainty that results from China's progressive integration into the global IT industry, the study culminates in a plea for China to experiment further with new, more market-driven, and flexible approaches to industrial policy.

Part One: Unresolved Friction between State and Market Explains Why China Is Still Playing Second Fiddle in Semiconductors

1. CURRENT STATUS—CHINA'S ACHIEVEMENTS ARE OVERSHADOWED BY PERSISTENT WEAKNESSES

To understand the motivations behind China's new push in semiconductors, it is useful to take stock of China's current status in the semiconductor industry.

Achievements

The achievements are impressive for a country that, before 2000, was considered to be a minnow in this industry. The country's rise as the global electronics factory drastically increased China's demand for semiconductors.

China today is the world's largest assembler and manufacturer of information and communications technology (ICT) and other electronic equipment, with over half of the world's electronics production.[24] In 2013, China accounted for about 81 percent of the global production of mobile phones, 63 percent of personal computers, 57 percent of color televisions, 60 percent of LCD TVs, and 75 percent of digital cameras.[25]

Since 2005, China has become the largest and fastest-growing semiconductor market in the world. In 2013, China's semiconductor consumption market grew by more than 10 percent (compared to a worldwide semiconductor market growth of 4.8 percent). This has increased China's share in world semiconductor consumption to almost 56 percent (up from less than 19 percent in 2003). In 2014, China accounted for half of the $335.8 billion global semiconductor market.[26] As a result, China is by far the most important market for US semiconductor firms.

However, nearly three-quarters of all the semiconductors consumed in China (based upon revenue value) are re-exported as components of exported electronic systems that are produced in China, primarily by foreign companies from the United States, South Korea, Japan, and Taiwan.[27] Until 2013, this has created, in effect, a closed-loop supply chain that Chinese firms are not a part of. Buying decisions for integrated circuits (ICs) consumed in China were mostly made in Taiwan, South Korea, the United States (for mobile devices), Japan, and Singapore.[28]

As a result, the demand from Chinese electronic equipment vendors has only played a limited role in China's huge and rapidly growing semiconductor market. But, as we will see in Part Three of the study, this is beginning to change, as Chinese vendors of mobile devices, and in particular smartphones, have now become important drivers of China's semiconductor demand.

Another important achievement is the rapid growth of China's IC design industry, from $200 million in 2001 to $13.2 billion in 2013 (growing by 33 percent from 2012). As a result, the share of IC design in China's semiconductor industry has increased from 14 percent in 2010 to 20 percent in 2013.[29] In fact, IC design has consistently been the fastest-growing segment of China's semiconductor industry, and it continues to grow. For instance, the number of Chinese IC design companies has increased from 518 in 2012 to 683 by the end of 2013. That phenomenal increase of 165 net additional IC design houses during 2013 is by far the largest net increase in the last ten years.[30]

Chinese IC design companies are also at long last beginning to emerge as competitors in the global IC design industry. In 2014, there were nine Chinese companies among the top-50 fabless companies, as compared to only one company in 2009.[31] In total, the Chinese fabless IC suppliers held 8 percent of the top-50 fabless IC market ($80.5 billion) in 2014 and currently hold twice as much top 50-fabless IC market share as European and Japanese companies combined.[32]

There are, however, serious limitations in terms of scale and product range. The more than 600 Chinese IC design companies that have sprung up may have combined annual sales exceeding NT$400 billion (about US$13.2 billion)—beating Taiwan's IC design sector—but most of them are "one-generation champions" that are broken up by their founders after going public and lack staying power.[33] With the exception of a few industry leaders (such as Huawei's HiSilicon affiliate, ZTE Micro (ZTE); Spreadtrum; RDA Microelectronics (RDA);[34] Rockchip; and a few others), most Chinese IC design firms are too small to invest in sophisticated design capabilities and are bound to focus on low-end applications for mature and standardized products.[35]

Important qualitative weaknesses that constrain the growth of China's IC design industry include a narrow focus on consumer products, especially low- and middle-end products such as color TVs, sound systems, clocks, electronic toys, small home appliances, and remote controls. As long as China depends on these mature and relatively standardized products, this will constrain China's R&D and capability development in IC design.

Over the last few years, the government has promoted the development of an eight-core microprocessor that departs from the established design architectures of Intel and AMD. The intention is to secure China's capability of making its own processors in order to reduce technology dependence on those core components. Introduced at the San Francisco IEEE International Solid-State Circuits Conference (ISSCC) in February 2012, China's flagship microprocessor Godson-3B1500 features 32-nanometer process technology, which is considerably behind the leading edge. In addition, the 40-watt Godson central processing unit (CPU) is targeted for desktops, laptops, or servers, and a modified version (the so-called ShenWei processor SW1600) can be used for supercomputers. However, this type of processor does not address the low energy-consumption needs of China's booming mobile devices market.[36]

This neglect of basic market requirements is arguably more pronounced in a related project, the development of an indigenous operating system (OS) to replace Windows and Android for running China's desktop and mobile devices. That project appears to represent more of a traditional technology protectionist bias. Led by Ni Guangnan, a former chief technology officer of Lenovo and an academician of the Chinese Academy of Engineering, the OS Development Alliance, established in March 2014, seeks to benefit from the government ban on the procurement of Windows 8. However, the alliance faces many problems, including "a lack of research funds and too many developers pulling in different directions."[37] And according to interviews conducted by *EETimes* with domestic handset vendors and fabless companies, "it's far from clear how quickly and seriously the Chinese OS will attract local Chinese technology companies whose business is supplying products not only to domestic consumers but to the global marketplace."[38]

More important achievements, however, are IC designs developed by Spreadtrum and RDA for lower-end smartphones, and IC designs for mid-range tablets developed by Rockchip.[39] A vital achievement in technology terms is HiSilicon's introduction in late September 2014 of the world's first multicore networking processor for next-generation wireless communications and routers, and the fact that Taiwan Semiconductor Manufacturing Co. (TSMC), Taiwan's global foundry leader, has agreed to produce this device using the leading-edge technology, 16-nanometer FinFET fabrication.[40]

Despite these developments, China's IC design capabilities overall continue to lag far behind the United States, Japan, Taiwan, and South Korea, in terms of both process technology and design line width. In addition, China lacks strong domestic suppliers of electronic design automation (EDA) tools and software and domestic licensors of IC design-related intellectual property.

Another noteworthy achievement of China's semiconductor industry is the successful diversification into optical devices (especially LED), sensors, and discrete devices, with China now approaching self-sufficiency. By 2013, for the first time, a Chinese supplier entered the top-10 ranking of packaged LED makers, competing with leading global players such as Nichia, Osram, and Samsung.

Of particular interest, however, is the surge of China's semiconductor assembly, packaging, and testing (APT) industry, which has become the global market leader. Measured in terms of value added, production revenue, employees, and manufacturing floor space, China's APT industry has now moved ahead of Taiwan and Japan.[41] The focus on APT clearly stands out as a pragmatic and successful strategic decision. In the first place, a huge market exists for APT services. In addition, while entry barriers are lower than for front-end IC fabrication, the technological requirements are considerable, providing a cost-effective entry strategy for Chinese firms to build up their management and technological capabilities.[42]

Persistent Weaknesses

China's achievements in the semiconductor industry are impressive. Yet, they cannot hide the fact that, despite massive government efforts to build indigenous innovation and production capabilities, China still plays a very limited role in semiconductor production, IC design, and as an innovator. Of particular concern is the large and growing gap between semiconductor consumption and production. From $5.7 billion in 1999, this gap has ballooned to a record $108.2 billion in 2013, and it is projected to increase to $122 billion in 2015. According to Chinese sources, only 8.2 percent of China's total semiconductor consumption in 2013 (estimated at $145 billion) is supplied by Chinese semiconductor firms.[43]

As a result, up to 80 percent of the semiconductors consumed in China-based electronics manufacturing needs to be imported. As about 75 percent of these electronics end products are exported, this requires growing imports of advanced ICs that satisfy the demanding performance requirements of overseas markets. In fact, China's trade deficit in semiconductors doubled since 2005 to $138 billion in 2011. And in 2012, the value of China's semiconductor imports ($232.2 billion) even exceeded the amount it spent on crude oil ($221 billion).

Equally important are qualitative weaknesses. China's patent applications for semiconductors are growing, but China still has a long way to go to catch up with the United States. While China's share of worldwide semiconductor technology-focused patents increased from 13.4 percent in 2005 to a peak of 21.6 percent in 2009, it has since declined to 14 percent in 2012.[44] There are, of course, widespread doubts in the literature that growth in patent applications necessarily indicates that a country's innovation capacity is improving.[45]

China continues to lag behind in innovation, especially for advanced semiconductors. The United States is way ahead in multicomponent semiconductors (MCOs)[46] and multichip packages (MCP)[47]—the two semiconductor product groups that are at the heart of the current stalemate in negotiations to expand the Information Technology Agreement (ITA).[48] And Qualcomm, a global fabless IC design company, leads in "multimode" wireless communication chips that integrate various wireless standards (including the 4G LTE standard, derived from China's TD-SCDMA standard).

In short, China's IC design industry still has a long way to go to catch up with the leading IC design industries in the United States, Japan, the European Union (EU), Taiwan, and South Korea. There is no Chinese IC design company in sight that might be able to challenge current global industry leaders. According to a recent industry panel on China's IC design industry, "the center of gravity for chip design has not shifted to China. Despite a few well-known Chinese companies like HiSilicon and Spreadtrum, the top-10 fabless companies are all in the United States, Taiwan, or Japan. These companies are spending billions of dollars to invest in new development."[49]

As for wafer fabrication, China continues to play second fiddle. While wafer fabrication has moved to East Asia (primarily South Korea and Taiwan),[50] China's 2015 share of total worldwide semiconductor wafer production is projected to remain below 11 percent. Global IC industry leaders such as Intel, Samsung, and Hynix dominate China's wafer fabrication. In 2014, US semiconductor firms accounted for nearly 60 percent of China's $91.6 billion semiconductor market.[51] This highlights a fundamental imbalance between the United States and China in the semiconductor industry. While US semiconductor firms in 2014 accounted for 51 percent of worldwide semiconductor sales, their Chinese counterparts only had a 4 percent share).[52] On the other hand, HiSilicon, an affiliate of Huawei and China's largest semiconductor supplier, was ranked 24 in IHS Technology's April 2014 list of top suppliers (moving up from the position of 28 in 2013).[53]

Chinese foundries are lagging two generations behind in process technology and wafer size. In fact, China has made substantial new investments in wafer fabrication plants, but these plants are using older technology and used equipment, reflecting China's focus on LED and other applications that do not require leading-edge semiconductors. Further, as demonstrated in a case study of Semiconductor Manufacturing International Corporation (SMIC), China's leading foundry, Chinese foundries lack process innovation capabilities.[54]

As of December 2014, only 7 percent of global 300-millimeter wafer capacity is based in China. Of that, only 2 percent is owned by Chinese firms.[55] The vast majority of capacity in China is controlled by foreign firms, especially Intel, Samsung, Hynix, Powerchip, and United Microelectronics Corporation (UMC). According to *IC Insights,* China lags far behind Taiwan and South Korea as a market for exports of semiconductor manufacturing equipment by US firms. No Chinese firms are among the 20 semiconductor sales leaders during the first half of 2015. And no Chinese firms are among *IC Insights'* top-10 analog IC suppliers.[56]

In short, Chinese foundries have a long way to go before catching up with the leading Taiwanese foundries, which have 60 percent share of worldwide 2013 foundry revenues versus less than 5 percent for leading Chinese foundries[57]. This describes a fundamental challenge for China's new policy to strengthen its semiconductor industry: China's domestic semiconductor manufacturing (i.e., wafer fabrication) technology and capabilities have failed to keep up with the country's IC design capabilities and needs.

2. ROOT CAUSES—"INDIGENOUS INNOVATION POLICY" COLLIDES WITH "GLOBAL TECHNOLOGY SOURCING" NEEDS OF CHINESE SEMICONDUCTOR FIRMS

The semiconductor industry has been a poster child of China's innovation policy as codified in the **Strategic Emerging Industries (SEI) plan** published in 2012.[58] Yet what explains the fact that, despite massive government efforts to catch up and forge ahead in semiconductors, China still plays a quite limited role in semiconductor fabrication, IC design, and, most importantly, as an innovator?

To explain this puzzle, it is necessary to examine two conflicting innovation strategies that coexist in China's semiconductor industry, reflecting an unresolved friction between state and market. On the one hand, there is the government's **Indigenous Innovation Policy,** which seeks to correct the failure of the earlier FDI-based export strategy to develop and enhance absorptive capacity and innovation capabilities of Chinese firms. On the other hand, there are the global technology sourcing strategies of Chinese semiconductor firms, which are eager to source core technologies and capabilities from global industry leaders.[59]

Indigenous Innovation

Indigenous innovation was adopted as a policy in the **Medium- and Long-Term Plan for Science and Technology Development 2006–2020** (MLP),[60] which provided a domestically controlled alternative for developing core technologies that are (asserted to be) unavailable on the international marketplace. It should be stressed that "indigenous innovation" policies do not advocate technological autarchy. Global technology sourcing and the integration of acquired technologies into new technological solutions are explicitly mentioned in the MLP as types of indigenous innovation.

However, the policy's main objective is to shift the balance from global technology sourcing via FDI to domestic R&D, with the goal of replicating as much as possible the semiconductor value chain in China. An important objective is to leverage control of intellectual property in order to reduce licensing fees and to extract rent. In the end, the indigenous innovation policy seeks to "change the rules of the game to fit China," to break the technological dominance of the West, and to strengthen the country's position in the cybersecurity war.[61]

The MLP sets as a target the increase in domestic R&D expenditures relative to expenditure on technology imports, which is unlikely to be compatible with aggressive global technology sourcing. Moreover, the strong stress on indigenous innovation undoubtedly discourages firms from developing deep partnership strategies with foreign firms, which are leaders in important core technologies. In any case, the actual outcome, as figure 1 shows, is that China has dramatically increased domestic outlays for

R&D, while expenditures for technology imports have grown much more slowly. Between 2000 and 2010, domestic R&D increased by nearly a factor of ten (in dollar terms, converted at exchange rates), while technology import expenditures increased by about 40 percent. China obviously needs to strengthen domestic R&D, but the current indigenous innovation policy seems to have led to some considerable overs-shooting.

Figure 1. Expenditure on Domestic R&D and Technology Import

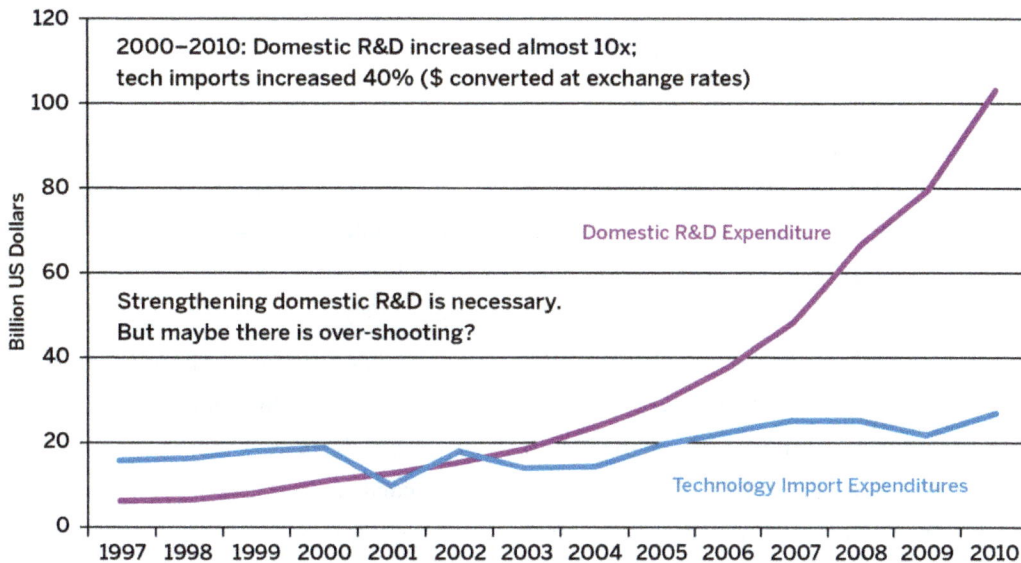

Source: Ernst and Naughton 2012; China Statistical Yearbook 2012.

In an interesting critique of indigenous innovation policy, Chen Tain-Jy argues that a basic proposition of these policies is not supported by China's experience in the IC design industry.[62] According to Chen, traditional policies draw on Joseph Schumpeter's proposition that large firms with monopoly power are more likely to innovate than small and competitive firms.[63] Yet, drawing on evidence from three sectors of China's IT industry—consumer electronics, computers, and mobile communications—Chen suggests that "national champions in fact impede rather than facilitate indigenous innovation. National champions are more concerned with protecting their market shares than engaging in innovation. In a technology-lagging country like China, foreign technologies are a more effective means of protecting market share than indigenous technologies, and market power provides national champions with good leverage when importing foreign technologies."[64]

Chen concludes that the market power of national champions does not necessarily lead to innovation. "Contrary to the Schumpeterian hypothesis, firm size does not prompt national champions to engage in indigenous innovation. In fact, large firm size provides national champions with the advantage of importing foreign technologies, and not innovation. While size allows them to spread the costs of technology imports, size provides no such advantage in terms of creating indigenous technologies. This is because indigenous technologies have only limited market applications even in a large Chinese market, given the predominance of foreign technologies in relation to the mainstream products."[65] Thus, market power may actually become "an impediment to the adoption of state-created indigenous technologies."[66]

In short, while China's indigenous innovation policy has no doubt boosted the infrastructure and capabilities within China's semiconductor industry, this massive quantitative push is only part of what is needed. An important qualitative shortcoming of China's indigenous innovation policy is a failure to adjust its top-down organization to the dramatic changes in markets and technology that have transformed the semiconductor industry, both in the global semiconductor value chain and with the rise of private firms in China.

3. NEW OPPORTUNITIES FOR GLOBAL TECHNOLOGY SOURCING

China's semiconductor industry is deeply integrated into the global semiconductor value chain through markets, FDI, and investment. In the demand chain, for instance, end users, global brand name companies, and electronic manufacturing service providers define performance and cost. In the supply chain, design tool vendors, design services, materials vendors, equipment vendors, and semiconductors producers (including foundries) are important sources of technology and capabilities.

The process of vertical specialization started decades ago, as the semiconductor industry reorganized around so-called "fabless IC design companies," which sent their designs to be made into silicon-based products at "pure-play foundries" (IC contract manufacturers).[67] While a few of the largest integrated device manufacturers, such as Intel and Samsung, continued to combine IC design and fabrication (and thrived), most firms moved to the disaggregated model. Apart from moving wafer fabrication to Asia (as discussed before), this disintegration of the semiconductor value chain has also led to the spread of global innovation networks, shifting important segments of electronics system design and IC design to Asia.[68]

This massive process of slicing and dicing the global semiconductor value chain has substantially reduced entry barriers for newcomers, such as Chinese IC design firms. According to Dr. Leo Li, the chief executive officer (CEO) of China's leading IC design company, Spreadtrum, "the availability of IC design tools, semiconductor fab services, and open-source smartphone software [Android] allows Chinese firms to circumvent their weak spots and develop their strengths in hardware, IC design, and integration."[69]

In short, deep integration into the global semiconductor value chain enables Chinese firms to globally source technology and capabilities on a scale never thought possible before. In addition, as the global semiconductor industry critically depends on China's huge and rapidly growing market, this enhances China's bargaining power in negotiations about global technology sourcing.

Add to this fundamental changes in global end user markets for wireless communication chips, which have further transformed the organization of the global semiconductor industry and opened up new possibilities of an increasingly fine division of the IC design value chain.[70] One of these possibilities is the much larger space for Chinese firms to introduce new innovative and disruptive business models that foster and reward significant innovation in system and IC design. In fact, global value chain integration has enabled Chinese firms to disrupt the existing competitive order. This happened a few years ago when MediaTek, a leading chip design company from Taiwan, offered integrated baseband chipsets to Chinese handset producers in Shenzhen for low-cost counterfeits of branded handsets, the so-called "Shanzhai" handsets.[71]

With the introduction of Google's open-source smartphone operating systems Android, this disruption is now being repeated in the form of Shanzhai 2.0 budget smartphones. This enables Chinese IC design firms to concentrate on hardware design first, before developing and catching up in software design capabilities. At the same time, the availability of mature and inexpensive chipset solutions provided by Taiwan's Mediatek has further lowered the entry barriers, giving rise to a renaissance of China's Shanzhai sector, but this time the focus is on incremental innovations in low-cost smartphones.

As a result, a local ecosystem for budget smartphones is emerging that links IC designers, original equipment manufacturers (OEMs), and Chinese customers. The primary focus is on the China market, but increasingly other Asian emerging economies, such as India and Malaysia, are becoming important targets.[72]

Today, not only is China the biggest market for mobile handsets, with China Mobile being the world's biggest carrier by a margin. Since 2011, China has also emerged as the biggest market for smartphones, ahead of the United States, and third-generation (3G) mobile telecommunications is finally taking hold. In addition, massive investments are underway to accelerate the buildup of China's 4G network infrastructure. Together, these changes in markets and technology have created new strategic opportunities for Chinese IC design firms to upgrade their product portfolios, process technologies, and business models.

China's indigenous innovation policy is still struggling to adjust to these fundamental transformations in technology, as well as in global and domestic markets. As argued at the beginning of this study, two fundamental weaknesses constrain China's indigenous innovation policy. China's leadership continues to retain control over the selection of priority sectors, technologies, and areas of public development. Forging ahead in semiconductors by fiat explains the tremendous quantitative achievements, described before. However, such top-down industrial policy also comes at a heavy cost. As the state has only made limited efforts to engage in industrial dialogues with private industry, China's leadership has only incomplete knowledge of the real needs of diverse private Chinese firms in terms of global knowledge sourcing. This incomplete knowledge of who needs what in China's complex semiconductor innovation networks implies that however well-intentioned these top-down policies may have been when they were conceptualized, they may in the end fail to target the most important challenges. They may also end up providing incentives or subsidies that may not address the most important constraints faced by Chinese semiconductor companies in their attempt to move from catching up to forging ahead through innovation.

A second weakness of China's indigenous innovation policy has arguably amplified these negative unexpected effects—a deeply entrenched bias to control as many details of policy implementation as possible. This micromanagement bias obviously reflects vested interests of government bureaucrats. At the same time, there seems to be a real concern within the leadership that top-down control remains necessary in order to defend the country against challenges facing China's transition to innovation-led development, especially with regard to licensing costs and cybersecurity.

Those challenges are real and need to be addressed. But as China's innovation policy seeks to reduce those threats, there is less space for developing incentives and support policies that would allow Chinese semiconductor companies to reap the huge gains from trade and deep integration in global production networks, in terms of learning, the development of innovation capabilities, and of best-practice management techniques and institutions. Innovation theory shows that top-down policy implementation does not sit well with the messy and high-risk decisions that companies need to make when investing in new products, processes, and services. While China's indigenous innovation policy has undoubtedly strengthened important aspects of China's innovation system, its persistent top-down implementation bias has also confronted companies with unintended barriers to innovation, with the result that both domestic and foreign semiconductor firms may hesitate to engage in risky innovation.

4. THE VIEW FROM INDUSTRY

In interviews reported in an earlier paper[73], some of the Chinese IC design companies acknowledged that the indigenous innovation policy provides new opportunities (through government procurement and participation in China's TD-SCDMA standard) to gain market share against established global players. However, there also was a palpable sense of frustration about certain aspects of the indigenous innovation policy that these companies felt were constraining their efforts to engage in global technology sourcing.

In fact, many aspects of China's innovation policy collide with the needs of Chinese semiconductor firms. For them, commercial considerations are a primary concern. As late entrants, Chinese semiconductor firms struggle to survive and grow in a highly competitive global market that keeps changing at lightning speed and where technology often has unexpected disruptive effects. As time-to-market is critical, and as product cycles often are as short as a few months, Chinese firms strongly feel that they cannot wait for the results of domestic research on processors and other core devices, when leading-edge new technologies are readily available from foreign firms. In their view, competitive success requires quick access to leading-edge foreign technology and the development of complementary capabilities. Global technology sourcing rather than indigenous innovation is their preferred innovation strategy.

China's persistent innovation gap in IC fabrication and IC design implies that Chinese firms continue to need access to core technologies and capabilities from global industry leaders. In fact, Professor Wei Shaojun, one of the drivers of China's new policy on the semiconductor industry, emphasizes that collaboration between US and Chinese semiconductor companies is badly needed: "The most advanced technology is in the US, and the most experienced talent is in the US....But Chinese companies are closer to the end customers and they understand the domestic demands."[74]

Hence, global technology sourcing across the semiconductor value chain is of critical importance if Chinese semiconductor firms want to reap the strategic opportunities that current changes in markets and technology are creating in, for instance, wireless communications.

One particular concern is that while strategy and vision are developed by the top leadership and the central government, implementation is left to the local governments. Due to misaligned incentives that emphasize GDP growth above everything else, local government officials are generally impatient and always expectant of big breakthroughs immediately after an investment is made. There is often little understanding that it takes time to move from an idea to a competitive product. In addition, there is a tendency for top-down technology leapfrogging by fiat that neglects the enormous risks of ramping up complex technology systems in record time.[75] Furthermore, reflecting a lack of transparency and trust, administrators and government bureaucrats are seeking to design tighter and tighter controls, which frequently result in unrealistic deliverables and project schedules.[76]

5. PERSISTENT FRICTION

There are additional reasons for the friction between China's innovation policy and the global technology sourcing needs of Chinese semiconductor firms. China's leaders are firmly committed to indigenous innovation as the key to removing poverty and to accelerating China's catching up with the United States, the EU, and Japan. Indigenous innovation is considered essential not only for moving beyond the precarious export-oriented growth model. At stake really is the survival of the system.

But the implementation of this strategic vision is hampered by the fragmentation of China's innovation system, which involves diverse stakeholders with conflicting interests[77]. This is hardly surprising. Like most emerging economies, China's innovation system is constrained by multiple disconnects between research institutes and universities on the one hand and industry on the other, between civilian and defense industries,[78] between central government and regional governments, and between different models of innovation strategy.[79]

Other constraining features of China's indigenous innovation policy include the widely discussed quality problems in education; plagiarism in science and derivative research; a privileged treatment of SOEs in public R&D support, and procurement that neglects SMEs; lists of indigenous innovation products used for government procurement that focus on existing technologies, and hence stifle innovation; weak complementary capabilities (for instance, in the legal realm, in patent law, and in standardization); and weak coordination of complex innovation networks.

In the end, it is this friction between the current form of indigenous innovation policy and the global technology sourcing needs of China's semiconductors firms that defines the dual challenge for China's new policy on semiconductors: Is China adequately accounting for the unintended costs of its indigenous innovation policy, and are adjustments made accordingly? And does China's new push in semiconductors find, or at least experiment with, new ways to combine the benefits of both innovation strategies—indigenous innovation and global technology sourcing?

Part Two: China's New Push in Semiconductors—What Do We Know about Objectives, Strategy, and Policies?

On June 24, 2014, China's government issued the **Guidelines to Promote National Integrated Circuit Industry Development**, which spells out concrete and ambitious development targets for China's semiconductor industry.[80] This strategy has the support of the top leadership. The goal is to move from catching up to forging ahead in semiconductors, by strengthening simultaneously China's integrated circuit (IC) design industry and domestic IC foundry services.

How successful will this new strategy be in upgrading China's semiconductor industry through innovation? Foreign observers largely agree that this time round China's policy on semiconductors will work better than before, and that this will transform the global industry over the next few years. Officials with the Washington, DC–based Semiconductor Industry Association (SIA) have argued that this new policy was a serious effort and that key policymakers knew precisely what they wanted.[81] And officials of Semiconductor Equipment and Materials International (SEMI), which is the industry association for US semiconductor manufacturing equipment makers, argue that US and other foreign companies in China have little choice but to adjust their strategies to China's new semiconductor policy. According to Allen Lu, president of SEMI China,

China's semiconductor industry will expand dramatically.....China's new industry investment and government promotion policies represent major opportunities for China and global semiconductor companies. The global industry is closely watching the details of the policy and its implementation—both because of the resources China's government has dedicated and the potential impact to the global semiconductor manufacturing supply chain. It is anticipated that the new policies will exert a significant influence on China and the entire semiconductor ecosystem.[82]

For US semiconductor firms and producers of production equipment, gaining and maintaining access to China's large and rapidly growing market is the overriding goal. To some degree these firms are betting their future on the success of China's policies. Intel, for instance, now depends on China for one-fifth of its revenues, while Qualcomm relies on the China market for nearly half of its revenues.[83] In fact, US and other foreign firms are quite explicit that they would be willing to accede to Chinese demands to transfer technology and form joint ventures with its firms, if only they could expand or at least sustain their share of the China market. In short, leading global semiconductor companies seem to be resigned to "helping China grow domestic competitors in exchange for short-term market access."[84] Part Three of this study will address the role of foreign companies as an amplifier of China's policies, and examine whether foreign firms in some cases may actually provide more effective support than the government in expanding China's semiconductor value chain.

Here in Part Two, the analysis focuses on the objectives and strategy of China's new push in semiconductors and analyzes major policy initiatives. How realistic are the aforementioned optimistic expectations? Will China's leadership finally move away from top-down policies that, while conducive for catching up, may no longer be appropriate for the transition to an innovation-driven industry development?

1. BACKGROUND

A brief look at the origins of China's semiconductor industry might help to get a clearer picture. It is useful to recall that China's strategy to develop the semiconductor industry has experienced many changes in a relatively short period of time. Frequent vacillation between statist and more market-friendly policies reflect a tension between two conflicting objectives: As a latecomer to this industry, China needs to develop and upgrade a robust domestic production and innovation system, while at the same time Chinese firms are eager to reap the benefits of global knowledge sourcing through deep integration into the industry's global value chain.

In fact, until 2000, practically all of China's semiconductor companies were state-owned enterprises, foreign direct investment was heavily restricted, and decision making was controlled by the Chinese government. In June 2000, State Council Rule 18 brought an important shift in policy, with a new focus on reducing the role of SOEs, encouraging FDI, and offering tax incentives.[85]

Rule 18 expired in December 2010, and was succeeded by State Council Rule 4, as part of the Twelfth Five-Year Plan published in February 2011.[86] The new policies, set to expire in 2017, signal an important shift from an emphasis on quantitative growth of production capacity and output value growth to a focus on improving R&D capabilities for advanced technology. Rather than pouring funds indiscriminately into the industry in a "shotgun" approach, the focus now is on selectively supporting a small group of semiconductor firms with global market share and the capacity for technological innovation. In contrast to Rule 18, Rule 4 places much greater emphasis on pragmatic choices, based on a careful selection of which key bottlenecks and medium-term goals might be achievable with the current set of accumulated capabilities.

2. OBJECTIVES

China's new policy on semiconductors, as codified in the June 2014 **Guidelines,** seeks to address head on the following deeply entrenched weaknesses:

- A persistent funding gap prevents Chinese IC companies from financing investment and R&D.

- Firm-level innovation capabilities remain weak, and the industry continues to lag far behind the United States in its competitiveness and in its capacity to support innovation and China's cybersecurity.

- Little coordination exists between different parts of the IC industry value chain, with the result that industry development remains disconnected from market demand.

- Most importantly, the **Guidelines** single out the large and growing gap between semiconductor consumption and production as a critical roadblock to catching up and forging ahead in this industry.

For China's leadership, the resultant growing pressure on the trade balance defines an important objective of the new policy for semiconductors: to reduce the consumption/production gap through selective import substitution. It is reported that by 2020, the government's goal is to push the share of Chinese semiconductor companies filling the needs of China's semiconductor consumption to 50 percent, or as close to that level as possible.[87]

Such an ambitious target may not be realistic. However, as its manufacturing strategy shifts from exports to the domestic market, China may realistically expect to reduce the exported value of its electronic equipment production. In turn, this may open up at least some opportunities for reducing the imported content of its semiconductor consumption. There is, of course, no straightforward causal link. As discussed in Part Three of the study, much depends on the requirements of the electronics equipment manufacturers, in terms of performance, price, and timing. Equally important are the technological and management capabilities of China-based fabless companies.

To reduce the production/consumption gap through import substitution, the **Guidelines** describe fairly concrete targets for 2015, 2020, and 2030. In the fast-moving semiconductor industry, projections that extend beyond a few years should, of course, be treated with a grain of salt. Nevertheless, it is useful to document the expectations of China's leadership.

For 2015, the focus is on strengthening what could be called the IC design-foundry nexus.[88] By leveraging the demand pull from mobile devices (especially budget smartphones) to strengthen the IC design industry, the goal is to turn IC design into an engine of growth for China's IC foundry industry. In turn, the target for IC fabrication is to enable Chinese IC foundry services providers to upgrade from 40-nanometer to 32-nanometer and 28-nanometer process technology.[89] For IC assembly, packaging, and testing (APT), the 2015 target is that at least 30 percent of APT revenue should come from mid- to high-end packaging and testing technology.

The target for 2020 is to gradually increase China's local value added and to upgrade its position in the global semiconductor value chain. In addition, China should join global industry leaders in IC design for mobile devices, cloud computing, the Internet of Everything (IoE), and Big Data. Finally, by 2030, Chinese firms are expected to compete with global industry leaders across key sectors of the IC industry supply chain and create disruptive technological breakthroughs.

3. STRATEGY

China's new strategy to promote IC industry development has both a defensive element and a more assertive and self-confident element.

The Defensive View

The defensive view holds that China needs to respond to a combination of persistent domestic weaknesses and new threats to its security and international competitiveness resulting from global transformations.[90]

China's Ministry of Industry and Information Technology (MIIT), for instance, emphasizes that—despite rapid growth—Chinese IC companies generate low profit margins, and hence have limited means to finance investment. The company SMIC is mentioned as an example of this financial bottleneck: "In 2013, SMIC realized a record profit of about $170 million, but it needs to invest around $5 billion to produce a month's supply (50,000) of its 12-inch, 28-nanometer chips. TSMC, on the other hand, realized a net profit of $6.2 billion, which allowed it to cover its investments for more than six months."[91]

An equally important concern is that China's IC fabrication technology "remains two generations behind global leaders, and we are still dependent on imported equipment and materials."[92] As documented earlier in this study, Chinese foundries do, indeed, lag considerably behind in process technology and wafer size, and they have a long way to go to improve their absorptive capacity and process innovation capabilities. In addition, most Chinese IC design firms are too small to invest in sophisticated design capabilities.

China's new policy on semiconductors seeks to break this vicious cycle, where weak IC design capabilities feed into weak IC fabrication capabilities. According to Tsinghua University's Wei Shaojun, Chinese IC design houses must upgrade in order to secure access to limited foundry capacity. It is worthwhile quoting Dr. Wei's blunt statement:

As chip production becomes increasingly sophisticated and expensive, the number of customers dedicated chip contractors can fully support will become increasingly limited, giving control of production capacity added importance....Capacity is king [in the global foundry industry.]...If Chinese chip designers cannot squeeze into the global top 10, they will have trouble securing capacity....This predicament is of even greater concern to Chinese authorities than the high value of IC imports.[93]

Of particular concern for China's leadership is the persistent innovation gap in advanced semiconductors relative to the United States. According to MIIT, China continues to remain focused on its role as the "global electronics factory," while remaining weak in high value-added activities in IC fabrication, IC design, and software. An equally disturbing domestic weakness is the disconnect between IC design and domestic electronics manufacturing. In terms of policy implementation, MIIT highlights the deeply entrenched interagency rivalries, which give rise to a lack of coordination among different stakeholders in China's semiconductor industry.

Global transformations, from the perspective of China's government, create competitive pressure for China's semiconductor industry. In response to the global recession, developed countries have accelerated their structural adjustments, focusing on policies to enhance their international competitiveness. They all seek to expand exports, especially for high value-added industries in the high-tech sector.

In the view of China's leadership, the United States has now shifted to more aggressive industrial, innovation, and trade policies to retain its leadership in the semiconductor industry, which is considered to be one of the main drivers of economic growth.

From China's perspective, the semiconductor industry poses significant entry barriers for latecomers, as a limited number of leading firms maintain oligopolistic control in important market segments, such as Qualcomm and ARM for smartphone chipsets, Samsung for memory chips, and Taiwan's TSMC for semiconductor foundry services. In 2014, US semiconductor firms accounted for 51 percent of worldwide semiconductor sales, while Chinese companies only had a 4 percent share.[94] US producers of semiconductor manufacturing equipment accounted for 44 percent of the global market. And the "big three" in semiconductor fabrication (Intel, Samsung, and TSMC) accounted for around 60 percent of global capital expenditures for semiconductor facilities. Only these three firms have what it takes to build the next-generation facilities that can produce 450-millimeter wafers with leading-edge process technologies (20 nanometers and below).[95]

Chinese technology planners have studied the global semiconductor industry enough to conclude that this is an industry in transition, if not in turmoil. They observe that both for IC design and process technology, limitations to the existing technology trajectory are increasing. Traditionally, R&D in the semiconductor industry was based on Moore's Law, which observes that the number of transistors on a given chip can be doubled every two years,[96] and that the resultant "…[a]dvances in semiconductor technology have driven down the constant-quality prices of MPUs and other chips at a rapid rate over the past several decades."[97] Chinese planners realize that today this traditional approach to semiconductor R&D may no longer work—chips may still be getting smaller and faster, but further miniaturization no longer necessarily involves them getting cheaper, as the cost of R&D, extremely expensive production equipment, and software tools keep rising.[98]

At the same time, potentially disruptive new technologies transform the parameters of semiconductor demand and supply. Examples mentioned by MIIT include cloud computing, the industrial Internet, and the Internet of Everything. China's IC strategy assumes that these Internet-based networking technologies require complex multicomponent semiconductors (MCOs) in order to integrate systems on chips that consume little energy and that protect against cyberattacks. As became clear during negotiations for an expansion of the Information Technology Agreement (ITA), China's leadership considers the design and fabrication of these MCOs as an essential prerequisite for forging ahead in the semiconductor industry.[99]

In addition, Chinese technology planners realize that new materials, nanotechnologies, and 3D printing will further disrupt existing technology roadmaps. In some sectors of the semiconductor industry value chain, such radical changes in technology are expected to lead to a further strengthening of global oligopolies, where a handful of technology leaders control profits and sales, raising the barriers to entry for latecomers like China.

The Assertive View

In other sectors, however, Chinese technology planners expect that disruptive changes in technology may weaken existing global oligopolies. In the information technology (IT) industry, this was the case when the spread of mobile Internet-related devices eroded the erstwhile seemingly incontestable leadership positions of Intel and Microsoft in the personal computer (PC) market.

In the assertive view, global transformations in markets and technology, such as the ones discussed before, open up new opportunities for China to forge ahead in semiconductors, while domestic weaknesses call out for and provoke new policies to reduce or at least mitigate these weaknesses.

As for China's persistent domestic weaknesses, MIIT asserts that a Big Push policy response is required to strengthen the "weak parts of China's supply chain."[100] The Big Push approach—"make a firm decision and push forward"—constitutes a remarkable departure from the traditional focus of China's leadership on incremental policies.[101] Even more remarkable is that the Big Push approach is combined with a commitment to "the decisive role of the market in allocating resources."[102] In a way, it seems that the semiconductor industry is used as an early test case for the government to see how policies relying on the "decisive" role of the market might work in practice.

According to MIIT's Miao Wei, in China's new semiconductor strategy, "...[c]ompanies take the lead, with market orientation....Let the market determine the development of products, the technological path, and allow the market to unleash the vitality and innovative capacity of industry....Make better use of the government to create an environment for fair market competition, and strengthen and improve public service."[103] Specifically, mergers and acquisitions (M&A), both among Chinese companies and with global industry leaders, are now considered to be an important shortcut to strengthen financial resources, as well as management and technological capabilities.

As for global transformations in semiconductor markets and technology, there is a new confidence on the Chinese side that China now has a strong hand to play in international competition. Specifically, Chinese decision makers in government and industry seem to focus their attention on global transformations in semiconductor markets and technology, such as a demand pull from mobile devices, and new opportunities for China's catching up and forging ahead in trailing-node integrated circuit process technologies (28 nanometers and above).[104]

These global transformations might indeed provide new opportunities for China to move from catching up to forging ahead in the semiconductor industry. But as discussed in Part Three, China would need to move toward a bottom-up, market-led approach to "industrial policy" in order to seize fully these opportunities.

4. IMPLEMENTATION—WHAT IS DIFFERENT ABOUT THE NEW POLICIES?

Is China's government adjusting its support policies for semiconductors, drawing on multilayered industrial dialogues with private firms, both domestic and foreign? Or will policies again rely heavily on control and micromanaging investment decisions, and thus possibly waste the opportunities provided by global transformations in markets and technology?

Efforts to implement China's new semiconductor industry strategy gathered strength through support from Yu Zhengsheng, a prominent member of the current Standing Committee and a former party secretary of Shanghai.[105] Yu has long been involved in the development of China's electronics industry.[106] Yu nominated Vice Premier Ma Kai (who was chairman of NDRC from 2003 to 2008) to head China's new policies on IC industry development.

Tax breaks and subsidies continue to play a role. In addition to keeping the tax breaks mentioned in the **State Council Document 4 (2011)** for IC design houses and foundries, the tax benefits have now been expanded to semiconductor testing firms. This means testing firms now also enjoy savings on corporate income, value added, and operation taxes.

At the same time, the government seeks to create new mechanisms to improve the efficiency of government financial support instruments, especially through the Ex-Im Bank and the China Development Bank. A particular emphasis is placed on debt-financing tools, to be issued especially for SMEs. Priorities include companies seeking to go public, R&D tax credits, and the improvement of loan insurance and credit insurance tools. In addition, the **Guidelines** emphasize efforts to strengthen tax support policies and use import tax exemptions for critical equipment, components, and materials that are needed for strengthening China's IC industry.[107]

Overall, however, the government is playing down the role of tax breaks and subsidies in the initiative, as those policies are easily attacked by foreign governments as violating World Trade Organization (WTO) anti-subsidy agreements.

Instead, the government emphasizes the central role to be played by two new policy initiatives:[108]

- An **IC Industry Support Small Leading Group**, chaired by Vice Premier Ma Kai, has been established for ministerial coordination of high-level national strategies.

- To improve investment allocation, a set of "market-driven" **regional and national IC Industry Equity Investment Funds** have been created "with limited government intervention."

To support these two key policies, the government (through NDRC) pursues a much more active anti-monopoly policy to reduce market abuse by IT companies. If such anti-monopoly policies are well designed, they could enhance the impact of the above two policies to upgrade China's semiconductor industry. Among US IT companies, prominent examples include the pressure on Qualcomm to reduce licensing fees, and investigations of business practices at Google, Apple, Microsoft, Cisco, and IBM. In Qualcomm's case, on February 9, 2015, NDRC imposed a fee of almost $1 billion for using its dominant position as a supplier of critical ICs to overcharge licensing fees for Chinese smartphone manufacturers.[109] According to Scott Kennedy, of the Freeman Chair in China Studies at the Center for Strategic and International Studies in Washington, D.C., "...[t]he Chinese government has credibility to pick on Qualcomm because of investigations into the company in other countries....But it also definitely fits their industrial policy goals if they can squeeze in lower licensing fees or other technology-sharing arrangements."[110]

NDRC's anti-monopoly policy is controversial—multinational executives and industry associations believe the NDRC is deliberately targeting foreign companies. In fact, data compiled by the *Financial Times* show that foreign companies or their joint ventures have paid almost 80 percent of the RMB$3 billion (US$490 million) in anti-monopoly penalties handed down by the NDRC since 2011. However, half of those RMB$2.4 billion in fines for foreign companies was assessed against 10 Japanese auto parts makers who admitted in August 2014 to price collusion. In addition, NDRC argues that its price supervision and anti-monopoly bureau is too inexperienced and understaffed to organize a conspiracy against foreign companies, although they are now recruiting new staff.[111]

At the same time, there are efforts to strengthen the role of trade diplomacy as a necessary complement of the above industrial support policies for the semiconductor industry. During the recent round of negotiations to expand the product list of the Information Technology Agreement (the so-called ITA-2), China seems to have experimented with a combination of delay tactics and a slowly evolving—and, in the end, surprisingly successful—strategy of co-shaping the conclusion of an expanded ITA, which took place on July 24, 2015.[112]

The IC Industry Support Small Leading Group

On November 29, 2013, China's Semiconductor Industry Association announced that China's State Council was to establish an **IC Industry Support Small Leading Group.**[113] An important objective of the leading group is to reduce interagency rivalries in order to improve strategy coordination and to mobilize and consolidate resources. A consulting commission that reports to the leading group acts as a think tank to assess policy measures, and to suggest solutions and adjustments in policies. The goal is to speed up government response time and to improve the capacity for flexible response by navigating around entrenched bureaucratic hurdles and rigid regulations. An additional function of the leading group seems to be to mobilize and consolidate public and private resources through public-private partnerships.

Leading groups have a long tradition in China as a tool to act against or mitigate the silos within the government, which bedevil the implementation of strategies laid out by the leadership. To bypass bureaucratic inertia and interagency rivals, the State Council occasionally establishes such "leading groups" of high-level officials to improve coordination across China's many ministries and other government organizations.[114]

In the IT sector, various leading groups have been established since the 1980s to issue key strategies and guidelines for the electronics industry.[115] Today's **IC Industry Support Small Leading Group**, however, displays some interesting new features in terms of organization and governance. On the one hand, there is continuity. Like in earlier periods, this leading group gains leverage from the direct involvement of China's top leadership. When the "908" and "909" projects were implemented in the 1990s, giving rise to the establishment of the Huahong-NEC joint venture, then Vice Premier Hu Qili was in charge.[116]

A similar pattern is repeated in today's IC Industry Support Small Leading Group, where Vice Premier Ma Kai acts as chair, and prominent local government leaders such as Beijing Vice-Mayor Zhang Gong play active roles. Participants include key players from four powerful ministries (MIIT, MoST, MoF, NDRC), top industry leaders, and senior academics with an established research and patenting record. For instance, Zixue Zhou, the chief economist at the vice-ministerial level of MIIT is one of the chief architects of the new China IC initiatives that led to the establishment of the China National IC Industry Fund. Or take Wenwu Ding, the former director-general of MIIT in charge of the semiconductor industry, who is now the CEO of the newly formed China National IC Industry Fund.

In addition, it seems that the expertise of participants from industry and research institutes has substantially improved. It is now more common to have experts who have studied and worked abroad and are internationally well-connected. Take the example of Dr. Wei Shaojun, who played an active role in drafting China's new IC industry policy. As dean of the Microelectronics Institute at Tsinghua University and president of the China IC Design Association, Wei is well-connected within leadership circles. He studied and worked in Belgium, and is internationally recognized and respected as both a frequent speaker at the Global Semiconductor Alliance (GSA) and as a key Chinese delegate to the World Semiconductor Council. Chinese experts like Wei know the international scene well, and are familiar with the intricacies of the global semiconductor industry value chain, which gives them a better understanding of what policies might work in this knowledge-intensive and highly globalized industry.

In short, while the institution of a leading group is not new for China, it nevertheless seems that some new wine is now being filled into these old bottles.

Regional and National IC Industry Equity Investment Funds

Arguably the most interesting new policy initiative is the announcement by MIIT and NDRC of the establishment of the **National IC Industry Equity Investment Funds**, endowed with RMB$120 billion (US$19.5 billion) over a three- to five-year period, to be complemented by a series of **Regional IC Industry Equity Investment Funds.**

Table 1 provides information on the structure and the investors of the initial national fund. It is noteworthy that so-called "societal funds," or private equity investment funds, are responsible for 36 percent of the national fund.

Table 1. Initial National Fund: RMB 120bn ($19.5bn)/3–5 Years — Structure & Investors

Investor	Amount (RMBbn/%share)
MoF	36 (30%)
China Development Bank	32 (26%)
Beijing E-Town Capital & municipal government	10 (8%)
"Societal funds" (non-governmental)	42 (36%)

Note: Wuhan, Shanghai, Shenzhen to follow the Beijing Fund model.
Source: USITO 2014, quoting data from E-Town Capital website.

More recently, MIIT announced that the Chinese government expects to invest as much as US$161 billion (RMB$1 trillion) over the next 10 years—a significant boost for its nascent semiconductor industry.[117] By comparison, however, US semiconductor firms spent more than $400 billion on R&D and capital expenditures for 2004–2014.[118] It is unclear how comparable these two figures are. Nevertheless, the huge gap may raise the question of whether the projected Chinese semiconductor investment will be sufficient to accelerate China's transition from catching up to forging ahead in semiconductors. It also indicates that there is a lot of pressure to use these investment funds effectively. Chinese authorities, in fact, indicate that they intend to use the national funds very selectively, "…to acquire foreign technology and leveraging joint ventures with established global leaders for technology transfer."[119]

The idea behind the IC Industry Equity Investment Funds could signal an important break with previous policies. According to an industry observer who has requested anonymity, "this is the first time that the Chinese have set up a fund jointly with public investors and asked professional fund management companies to raise, invest, and manage the funds, in contrast to direct subsidy or investment in selected projects or companies." Under the new approach, the investment fund will take stakes in companies proportionate to the amount invested, and the fund manager will insist on a rate of return. The ultimate goal is to leverage the ownership structure to change corporate and industry structures.

At this stage, these are declarations of intent, and it may be advisable to take such claims with a grain of salt. One might wonder, for instance, to what degree the decision to establish an investment equity fund is primarily motivated by an attempt to avoid being accused of violating WTO anti-subsidy agreements. It is difficult at this stage to ascertain to what degree the involvement of IC Industry Equity Investment Funds represents a clear shift toward more market-driven investment allocation.

It is interesting to note that at the 2015 SEMICON China event, held March 17–19 in Shanghai, key figures of the global venture capital and private equity industry attended in large numbers and expressed great interest in the investment opportunities resulting from China's new semiconductor industry policy. For instance, speakers at the event's tech investment forum included Yongzhi Jiang, managing director of Goldman Sachs Securities in charge of M&A; Lip-Bu Tan, founder and chairman of Walden International;

and fund managers from CGP Investment, GM E-town Capital, Summit View Capital, and Shenzhen Capital.[120] The presence of those global funds and their local affiliates seems to indicate that fund managers have a relatively free hand, and that politically motivated investments may also be profitable.

Another way to assess whether the establishment of the **IC Industry Equity Investment Funds** signal a more professional approach would be to look at the selection of the fund managers and the discretion they will have in allocating funds.

Publicly available knowledge on these questions is limited.[121] We know that the primary purpose of the national fund is to mobilize private and public funding sources to reduce the investment bottleneck faced by domestic semiconductor firms. According to the **Guidelines**, the national fund covers the whole industry value chain (design, manufacturing, R&D, and commercialization and knowledge-intensive support services). The fund also is supposed to play a catalytic role in promoting industry consolidation through M&A among domestic firms and the acquisition of foreign firms that control important technologies or markets.

As for regional funds, some information is now in the public domain on the **Beijing IC Industry Equity Investment Fund**. More regional IC industry support plans have also been released since the summer of 2014, including those for Anhui Province, Suzhou, Hefei city government, Sichuan Province, and Gansu Province. However, none of these announcements provide details on the selection of fund managers and their degree of decision autonomy on allocating funds.

The Beijing IC Industry Equity Investment Fund

A closer look at the **Beijing IC Industry Equity Investment Fund** finds that two fund managers have been selected thus far:

- The main fund and the dominate sub-fund for equipment and manufacturing are to be managed by **China Grand Prosperity Investment (CGP)**.

- In June 2014, **Hua Capital Management Co., Ltd (HCM)**, a Chinese investment management company, was chosen to manage the chip design and testing fund under the Beijing government's 30-billion-yuan (HK$37.8 billion) Semiconductor Industry Development Fund.[122]

The underlying financial networks are complex and difficult to disentangle. While CGP is headquartered in Hong Kong, it is definitely not a global player.[123] But, according to CGP's Chinese website, they have a long history of managing investment funds in China.[124] Cheng Hairong, the chairman of CGP, has over 20 years of experience as an executive director and consultant in establishing and managing listed companies in Hong Kong. Cheng has deep knowledge of finance and investments in China's life sciences, biotech, energy conservation, tourism, trading, and finance sectors.[125]

CGP seems to have learned how to walk the fine line between adapting to the requirements of the government and, at the same time, making sure that the fund produces enough profits. One could argue that this type of Chinese fund manager just fits nicely with the implementation requirements set by the government. In short, while elements of the market are now introduced, the government can simultaneously continue to exercise control. An industry observer who requested anonymity provided a telling example of this hybrid model of Chinese-style fund management. In a meeting with the Beijing

Municipal Government, partners of the CGP fund manager were present, and displayed a "highly deferential behavior" vis-à-vis the government representatives.

In June 2014, Hua Capital Management Co., Ltd (HCM) was reported to take over the management of the Beijing sub-fund for IC design, packaging, and testing. Hua Capital Management Co., Ltd (HCM) is a private equity firm specializing in buyouts, based in Beijing. Funds managed by HCM include the Shanghai Pudong Science and Technology Investment Co. Ltd, a wholly state-owned limited liability company, established directly under the Pudong New Area government of Shanghai.[126]

According to industry observers, the real driving force behind HCM is Chen Datong, who is HCM's chairman as well as co-founder and managing partner of WestSummit Capital, a leading China-based global equity firm focused on helping high-growth technology companies access the China market.[127] Another major player is Liu Yue, the deputy chairwoman of HCM, who also has a wealth of experience in China's IC industry. Of particular interest is her role as an early investor in SMIC through Walden Capital, and her continuous involvement with SMIC.

HCM's president, Xisheng (Steven) Zhang, started out in 1994 as a post-doctorate researcher at Uuniversity of California, Berkeley, worked his way into senior management positions at Agilent Technologies and Silicon Valley start-up IC design companies, and joined Beijing-based private equity investment company WestSummit Capital in 2013. Zhang has over 20 years industry experience in semiconductors, and in managing start-up companies in Silicon Valley and in Beijing.

Based on this information, one might conclude that HCM qualifies as a professional fund manager with considerable knowledge of key aspects of the semiconductor industry value chain, especially related to IC design. In the view of the United States Information Technology Office (USITO), the use of professional investment fund managers, as opposed to government subsidies or investment, "suggest a new approach to industrial policy that focuses on building a strong and sustainable investment environment in China."[128] But a final assessment has to wait until more information is available on how funds will ultimately be deployed.

For instance, while selecting private fund managers might seem to indicate a stronger role for the market, this may actually not be the case if the selected company (i.e., CGP) owes its selection to its close personal connections to the leadership. It is important to establish who makes the key decisions on the allocation of funds—bureaucrats or technocrats with deep industry knowledge.

But it is useful to dig a little bit deeper. The co-founders of Hua Capital include China Fortune-Tech Capital Co., Ltd and Tsinghua Holdings Co., Ltd.[129] China Fortune-Tech Capital is an equity investment management company, established by SMIC, China's leading semiconductor foundry[130] and an independent third party. The initial registered capital of China Fortune-Tech Capital is RMB$6 million, with 75 percent contributed by SMIC. China Fortune-Tech Capital manages SMIC's wholly-owned investment fund China IC Capital Co., Ltd. This fund has an initial investment of RMB$500 million and an operating period of 15 years, focusing on investing in IC funds and IC projects. Both China IC Capital and China Fortune-Tech Capital were set up in 2014 in response to the government's new policies in the semiconductor industry. And both companies are operated by Gao Yonggang, SMIC's chief financial officer and executive vice president, who is China Fortune-Tech Capital's chairman and the driving force behind China IC Capital.

One of China Fortune-Tech Capital's tasks is supporting local IC fund establishment and management. To realize this responsibility, China Fortune-Tech Capital founded Hua Capital with Tsinghua Holdings Co., Ltd, targeting the Beijing IC sub-fund. Besides this, China Fortune-Tech Capital also engages in the Shanghai fund establishment and management. In other words, SMIC, China's semiconductor foundry, is involved in both the Shanghai fund and the Beijing fund.[131]

As for the national fund, Beijing Unis Communication Technology Co., Ltd (北京紫光通信科技集团有限公司) is one of its eight founders. Beijing Unis Communication Technology has two shareholders: Tsinghua Holdings Co., Ltd (13.22 percent) and Tsinghua Unigroup (81.78 percent).

The impact of the above relationships and links on the effectiveness of the funds remains to be seen. But one thing is clear by now: SMIC and Tsinghua Unigroup, the Chinese giants in the IC manufacturing and IC design industries, respectively, are both active in China's national and local IC investment funds. This is in line with China's effort to create global firms that are large enough to compete with industry leaders, especially from the United States. Another Chinese semiconductor company that participates in the national IC investment fund is China Electronics Corporation (CEC), a big SOE and the parent holding company of Shanghai Belling and Shanghai Huahong, two important Chinese semiconductor firms.

The fact that two major Chinese semiconductor firms, SMIC and CEC, are both actively involved in the management of the presumably private IC equity investment funds raises doubts as to what degree these funds are really much different from China's old direct subsidy method. More case study research is required to resolve this issue.

Another unresolved question is whether the availability of IC industry equity funds will again lead to a competitive race that pits Beijing against Shanghai, Shenzhen, etc., with the result of duplicative investments that will end up giving rise to overcapacity. Furthermore, are there signs that policy decisions are less constrained by elaborate priority lists of "indigenous innovation" products and technologies? If these lists were still important, this would indicate that nothing much has changed.

In any case, the establishment of the IC Industry Equity Investment Funds certainly does not imply that China is converging to a US-style, market-driven policy approach. Instead of a radical shift away from the traditional investment model used during the catching-up phase, a more likely outcome is the development of a *hybrid* model that seeks to combine the logic of equity investment fund management with the objectives of China's IC development strategy.

Part Three: Upgrading Prospects—Economic Reasons for a Bottom-up, Market-led Industrial Policy

1. PERCEIVED OPPORTUNITIES[132]

China's leadership is very conscious that the United States is way ahead in advanced semiconductors and that China has a long way to go to close this gap. At the same time, however, the policy documents that define China's new policies for semiconductors also convey a new sense of optimism. Global transformations in semiconductor markets and technology are no longer only perceived as threats. In fact, China's technology planners now seek to identify pathways to innovation-led development for China's semiconductor industry that could benefit from those global transformations.

Specifically, their attention seems to focus on four global transformations, which are expected to create new opportunities for China to move from catching up to forging ahead in semiconductors: (a) the demand pull from mobile devices, (b) new opportunities for China's foundries in trailing-node semiconductor technologies, (c) changes in the IC foundry industry landscape, and (d) a new interest in strategic partnerships and mergers and acquisitions (M&A).

The following analysis will examine the economic rationale behind each of these four perceived opportunities and what factors might determine China's chances of success. While the opportunities are real, they all involve considerable uncertainty. An important finding is the precarious nature of these opportunities. In other words, basic parameters that determine how China will fare may change at short notice and in unpredictable ways. This implies that flexible policy implementation is required to cope with such uncertainty. If China wants to exploit the above opportunities, it needs to move toward a bottom-up, market-led approach to "industrial policy" guided by the principle of "smart specialization," as defined later in this study.

2. DEMAND PULL FOR MOBILE DEVICES AS A CATALYST FOR IC DESIGN

Chinese decision makers, both in government and industry, are convinced that China is now becoming a lead market for mobile devices, and hence can shape demand and technology trajectories. It is expected that the demand-pull from mobile devices will catalyze an upgrading of China's IC design industry. Chinese IC foundries, in turn, may be more motivated to invest in capacity expansion and technology upgrading once demand from local chip design houses increases. Quoting again MIIT's Miao Wei, China's market for mobile devices and for a wide variety of IT equipment is booming, and hence should provide "favorable conditions for China to leapfrog ahead of others."[133] As demand for low-end budget smartphones is driving volume growth, it is expected that China can leapfrog into emerging markets for sub-$50 smartphones.

China now is the world's largest smartphone market with almost 700 million smartphone connections, surpassing the United States (197 million), Brazil (142 million), India (111 million), and Indonesia (95 million).[134] Low-cost smartphones designed in China are flooding the market. In fact, Android phones designed in China now represent more than 50 percent of the global market.[135] In 2015, Chinese original equipment manufacturers (OEMs) are expected to design more than half of the world's phones.[136]

Data from the first half of 2014 indicate that smartphone shipments in China will exceed 400 million units in 2014, accounting for 93 percent of total mobile phone shipments in that market.[137] China now is the ultimate prize for global smartphone vendors. In the first quarter of 2014, China contributed 15.8 percent of Apple's total revenues, due primarily to sales of iPhone devices in China. In the second quarter of 2014, China accounted for 37 percent of global smartphone shipments—some 108.5 million units.[138]

Since 2008, the global market share of mobile phones produced in China has almost doubled, from 44 percent to 81 percent in 2013.[139] There is no doubt that China's policy to promote a third international standard for 3G (third generation) mobile communications has been an important enabling factor for China's success in the smartphone industry. China is now in a position to co-shape international mobile telecom standards. Both TD-SCDMA and TD-LTE standards have fostered the development of technical capabilities of IC design companies based in Greater China (Taiwan's MediaTek, and China's Spreadtrum and RDA).[140] Global industry leaders (Qualcomm, Nvidia, Marvell, and Intel) are all eager to tap into the thriving China market. As latecomers to China's TD (time-division) mobile telecom standards, these global firms are constrained by high fixed costs. But they have other huge advantages, such as superior technology and system integration capacity, and deep pockets due to the high licensing fees they can charge for their technology.

Figure 2 shows that in the first quarter of 2014, Chinese vendors accounted for a 50 percent share of the China market.

Figure 2. Domestic Vendors Stand Strong in China's Smartphone Market
% of Smartphone Shipments in China in Q1 2014

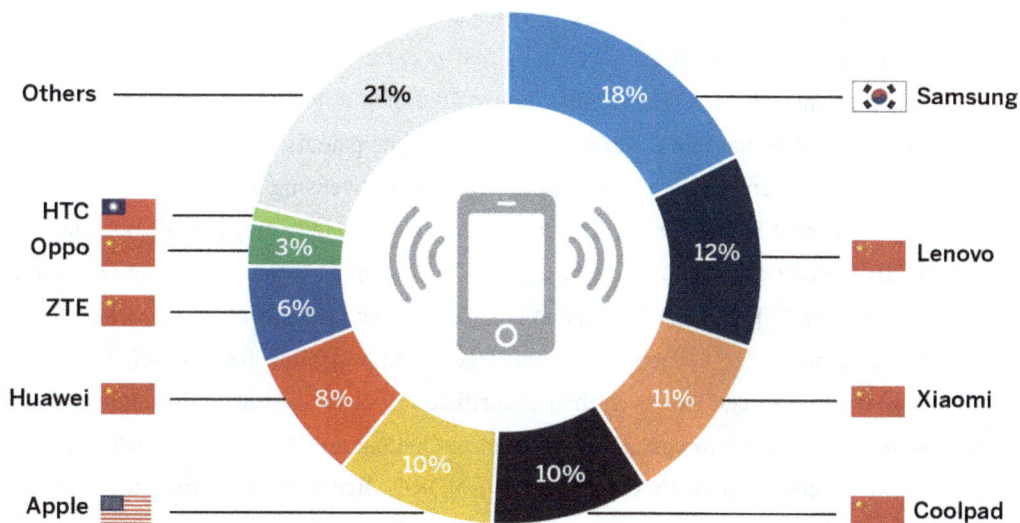

Chinese vendors have 50% share of China market

Source: Counterpoint - StatistaCharts.

How sustainable is this shift toward China becoming a lead market in mobile devices? Take Xiaomi, which has been catapulted from practically nothing a few years ago to the third-largest smartphone vendor in China[141] and fifth-largest globally. Xiaomi's handsets have achieved almost cult-like status in China, and the company was for a while the darling of global media and investors.[142]

After being valued at more than $45 billion and raising more than $1 billion in its latest round of funding, Xiaomi has joined Alibaba as the poster child of global investment funds. The stunning success of Xiaomi results from the fact that it sells smartphones for just half the price of the iPhone or Samsung's Galaxy phones, despite the fact that performance features and services are only slightly below the competitors.

For most observers, the key to success is innovative marketing. For example, to lower costs, Xiaomi cut out middlemen and distributors, selling only directly through its website. In addition, Xiaomi keeps each model on the market for two years—far longer than Apple does.[143] As component costs drop over the two-year period by more than 90 percent, Xiaomi maintains its original price and pockets the difference. This allows Xiaomi to use leading-edge components from Qualcomm, Nvidia, and Broadcom, and it outsources production to Foxconn, Apple's preferred contract manufacturer.

It is important, however, to emphasize that much of Xiaomi's success depends on the critical role played by a new form of strategic patenting that could destroy the value of patents not just in China, but also around the world.[144] The real story, in a nutshell, centers on Xiaomi's close links with the US smartphone chip vendor Qualcomm. Not only has Xiaomi received substantial equity investment from Qualcomm,[145] but Xiaomi's smartphones also use Qualcomm chips. Of critical importance is Qualcomm's cross-licensing model in China, which prevents patent fights from breaking out among Qualcomm's Chinese customers.[146]

This arrangement clearly benefits companies such as Xiaomi that have avoided investing in building up a broad patent portfolio. For instance, Xiaomi has filed at most 1,600 patent applications (most of which were filed in the last two years). But a mere 124 patents have been granted, with only 13 being inventions (the rest are design and utility model patents).[147] In comparison, Apple Inc. has been granted 1,149 patents in China, about half of which are inventions. Samsung Electronics has been granted 11,877 invention patents in China. And China's first-generation smartphone vendors Huawei and ZTE both have strong patent portfolios. Huawei has almost 30,000 mobile phone patents (with 7,000 registered in 2014 alone), and ZTE has more than 13,000 mobile phone patents. Both Chinese companies complain about "unfair" treatment as a result of Qualcomm's "cross-licensing model."

However, Xiaomi's patent-avoiding catching-up strategy may now be reaching its limits. On February 9, 2015, a year-long antitrust probe against Qualcomm by China's National Development and Reform Commission (NDRC) has culminated in an agreement that appears to constrain Qualcomm's "cross-licensing model."[148] Chinese owners of large patent portfolios like Huawei, ZTE, and Lenovo may benefit from this agreement. However, their immediate response was one of disappointment, arguing that the NDRC should have forced greater changes to Qualcomm's licensing procedures.

In any case, there is little doubt that the NDRC-Qualcomm resolution will leave Xiaomi exposed to potential legal challenges from large foreign patent owners, as well as its Chinese competitors.[149] Once Xiaomi will have to pay licensing fees, this will substantially raise its cost burden and further compress its already quite low profit margins, estimated to be around 1.8 percent at present. This raises the question whether the aforementioned massive capital injection by foreign investors will allow Xiaomi to force its way out of the patent trap, for instance, through massive investments in existing patent portfolios, with the help of patent monetization companies.[150]

Xiaomi's current response is to diversify into its own brand-name air purifiers and wearable devices. Analysts however discern a lack of coherence in the company's diversification efforts. In the end, as long as Xiaomi does not expand its patent portfolio, there is reason to doubt whether the company can sustain its earlier rapid growth. In fact, Xiaomi during 2015 has been hit by a flood of new lower-cost competitors who quickly copy key design features of Xiaomi's smartphones. In addition, there are increasing doubts that the move into global branding will succeed. The rise and fall of China's sportswear company Li-Ning, one of China's best-known brands, indicates possible limitations of a premature leap into global branding *without* a robust patent portfolio.[151]

The story of Xiaomi indicates that cutting corners to forge ahead without R&D and a growing patent portfolio may not be sustainable. According to a review of Xiaomi's smartphone technology,"Xiaomi has promise, but it is far from the world-dominating juggernaut that Western media makes it out to be."[152] Its success has been for 3G smartphones only, and not yet for leading-edge 4G/LTE devices.[153] In fact, China's 4G smartphone market has failed to surge as expected, and most Chinese vendors' domestic shipments did not achieve any growth.[154] It is too early to assess whether this slow growth of 4G smartphone demand indicates that the demand-pull effect from mobile devices is already being weakened.

If Chinese smartphone makers really want to move from catching up to forging ahead, they are faced with a very tight global oligopoly in this industry, and hence face severe upgrading barriers. Data for the first quarter of 2014 show that the combined global market share for the two dominant smartphone operating systems (Google's Android and Apple's iOS) has increased to 96.4 percent, leaving little space for latecomers like Xiaomi to differentiate themselves through alternative operating systems.[155]

This of course raises the question whether China really has a broad enough portfolio of core technologies and the ecosystem required to sustain the move toward becoming a lead market for mobile devices. Or are these expectations a bit premature?

In any case, both the Chinese government and multinational corporations (MNCs) clearly believe that the shift toward China becoming a lead market in mobile devices is real. As a result, MNCs are all trying to position themselves so that they can sustain market access in the future. It is this perception that seems to drive some of the other global transformations, discussed below, and especially the strategic partnerships between Chinese companies and global industry leaders discussed in Section 5.

3. THE TRAILING-NODE UPGRADING TRAJECTORY—NEW OPPORTUNITIES FOR CHINA'S SEMICONDUCTOR FOUNDRIES

Part One of the study described a fundamental challenge for China's new policy to strengthen its semiconductor industry: China's domestic semiconductor manufacturing (i.e., wafer fabrication) technology and capabilities have failed to keep up with the country's IC design capabilities and needs.

This raises the question about which of the following propositions should carry greater weight in shaping China's policy responses:

- China's technology gap in wafer fabrication today may matter less, as China's IC design houses can use a great variety of fabs and design services across Asia to tape-out their design needs, ranging from top-tier, leading-edge process technology foundries (like Taiwan's TSMC) down to highly specialized niche foundries for analog devices, which do not require leading-edge processes, or

- China's technology gap in wafer fabrication may, in the medium and longer term, substantially constrain efforts to upgrade its design industry because access to leading-edge foundry capacity may be denied during high-growth periods, and because proximity between design and wafer fabrication may still be critical for effective tape-out of leading-edge devices.

A survey of IC design firms in 2013 reported that proximity to foundries is perceived to be more important by Chinese IC design houses than by US design houses because Chinese firms have weaker technology capacity—and hence weaker bargaining power—in negotiations with large foundries like TSMC.[156]

That broad proposition, however, needs to be differentiated. Industry observers emphasize that the advantages or disadvantages of proximity to foundries differ, depending on the capability sets and bargaining power of different firms. The pros and cons also differ across product markets and market segments—design houses, for instance, that focus on analog, mixed-signal designs do not need access to leading-edge process technology, but are well-served with trailing-node process technology.

This study suggests that more specifics are needed about the precise nature of the policy challenge. One could ask, for instance, more targeted questions, such as: *As China-based design houses are ramping up 28-nanometer chip orders at TSMC, as reported in August 2014,[157] would they be better off if SMIC or any other China-based foundry could have a proven 28-nanometer process technology ready and could provide the full solution (fabrication of the design plus supporting design services that are especially important for latecomers like Chinese IC design firms)?*

China's technology planners, who have shaped the **Guidelines**, seem to have taken this more focused and pragmatic approach. Based on their research on the global semiconductor industry, the planners expect that significant and stable markets for trailing-node semiconductor technology (i.e., 28 nanometers and above) may open up new opportunities for Chinese foundries to gradually gain market share and improve their profit margins in these technologies. The primary beneficiary is expected to be SMIC, which, after all, is now the fifth-largest global foundry.

The underlying economics works roughly as follows: At this stage of the semiconductor cycle, trailing nodes (28 nanometers and higher) actually carry higher margins than the leading-edge technology nodes below 28 nanometers. This is so because most of the equipment used to produce trailing nodes is either partially or fully depreciated, so trailing nodes don't have the burden of depreciation. According to one observer, "trailing nodes may be returning higher margins because they are being manufactured in fully depreciated wafer fab facilities."[158]

On the other hand, producing devices at 20 nanometers and below is extremely expensive, resulting from the escalating cost of R&D, production equipment, and tools. There is an intense debate within the industry as to whether the cost of producing leading-edge devices will decline and, if so, at what pace. But it seems that the current consensus position within the industry is that barriers to such cost reductions will remain substantial for a considerable time.

Thus, second-tier foundries like SMIC may have a limited window of opportunity to compete in trailing-node technologies. They may be able to catch up with the leaders in technology and gradually gain share and improve their margin in these trailing nodes. Industry sources report that both SMIC and UMC actually have been gaining market share away from TSMC in these trailing nodes.[159]

This window of opportunity, however, may be closing soon. Once a second-tier foundry like SMIC is adding additional capacity, this will require new facilities with additional depreciation charges, which will reduce margins. And if more foundry capacity would be added, leading to excess capacity, the resultant cost increases would erode profit margins.

SMIC's management seems to bet that the trailing-node upgrading trajectory will work. But the challenge to achieve this goal will be formidable. According to industry observers, SMIC is two generations behind that of Taiwan Semiconductor Manufacturing Co. (TSMC), the world's largest contract chipmaker. In the *2013 IC Foundries Report*, SMIC has retained its position as the fifth-largest global IC foundry, and it has grown by 28 percent in 2013. However, in terms of its production capacity, SMIC remains a minnow compared to the three global industry leaders—Taiwan's TSMC and UMC, and US-headquartered Global Foundries.

In addition, SMIC's net profit is not even one-thirtieth of TSMC's, explaining why China's semiconductor foundry sector, without government support, lacks the capital needed to ramp up production and compete in the trailing-node processes. While the leading Taiwanese foundries (TSMC, UMC, and Powerchip) have a combined 60 percent share of worldwide 2013 foundry revenues, the combined share of China's SMIC and HHGrace is less than 5 percent.

Will SMIC Be Able to Narrow the Technology Gap?

According to the most recent *Global and China Wafer Foundry Industry Report, 2013–2014*, SMIC's major clients include Chinese IC design companies such as Spreadtrum, RDA, HiSilicon, GalaxyCore Inc., Rockchip, Allwinner Technology, GigaDevice, and Fudan Microelectronics. These companies use SMIC primarily for products that rely on government orders, such as social security cards, ID cards, SIM cards, and UnionPay cards. As a result, 40 percent of SMIC's revenue comes from the low-end 0.15/0.18-micrometer technology, while TSMC's revenue from below 65-nanometer technology accounted for 71 percent of the total.[160] In other words, many of SMIC's foundry service contracts are heavily dependent on the government, resulting in their lower efficiency.

China's technology planners nevertheless seem to be convinced that SMIC may be able to reap latecomer advantages for trailing-node technology (28 nanometers and above), provided, of course, that appropriate support policies are in place. The underlying economic rationale is aptly summarized by Tsinghua University's Wei Shaojun: "If the advanced processes…[i.e., below 28 nanometers]…cannot be brought into mass production on schedule, a major shortage of chips using the 28-nanometer process could emerge before 2017. That would give SMIC, which received 28-nanometer orders this year from Qualcomm, a chance to vault to the front of the pack. By 2017, global demand for the 28-nanometer process will be four million wafers a month. Right now, capacity hasn't even reached three million."[161]

China-based IC design companies (both domestic and foreign) are of critical importance, as they account for 40 percent of SMIC's revenues.[162] To address the real needs of its Chinese customers, SMIC pursues a flexible approach: "Over 28-nanometer process technology is fungible. In other words, those new 28-nanometer process lines are also capable of 40-nanometer products."[163]

According to SMIC's website, the company's 28-nanometer process technology was scheduled to be ready for foundry customers by the end of September 2014. A collaboration, announced in July 2014, between SMIC and Qualcomm on 28-nanometer wafer production in China is expected to accelerate this upgrading process.[164] In addition, SMIC seeks to diversify into potentially profitable specialty foundry niche markets for embedded EEPROM platforms[165] and micromechanical systems (MEMS).[166] For instance, SMIC developed an embedded EEPROM platform, which had been adopted by a majority of China's bankcard IC design houses. On microelectromechanical systems (MEMS), SMIC cooperates with Silicon Labs, a leading specialist fabless design company in the United States. [167]

According to an industry observer who has requested anonymity, SMIC's strategy has been focused on "stable niche markets (sensors) and trailing-node technologies plus services, something that TSMC was not interested in….It was a wise decision on SMIC's part to stop chasing Taiwanese [markets] and to seek growth opportunities beyond TSMC-dominated, leading-edge process markets."[168]

An Emerging Division of Labor in China's Semiconductor Foundry Industry

Thus far, China's trailing-node upgrading strategy for its foundry industry has produced two results: (a) an emerging 12-inch wafer fabrication cluster, centered on SMIC; and (b) an 8-inch foundry cluster, focused on another Chinese company, HHGrace. As discussed below in Section 4, it remains to be seen whether these achievements are sufficient to transform China's foundry industry into a credible global player.

The 12-inch wafer fabrication cluster, centered on SMIC

China has decided to develop a supply chain focused on 12-inch IC manufacturing fabs, centered on SMIC.[169] As part of this target, SMIC seems to focus on 12-inch wafer fabrication facilities with trailing-node process technologies of 28 nanometers and above.

In August 2014, SMIC and Jiangsu Changjiang Electronics Technology Co. Ltd (JCET) announced a joint venture for 12-inch bumping and related testing, to be established in Jiangyin National High-Tech Industrial Development Zone in China's Jiangsu Province. The joint venture can benefit from Jiangyin's unique location and mature industrial environment to quickly set up the 12-inch wafer bumping[170] and wafer testing production line, specifically for circuit probe (CP) testing.[171] In addition, the joint venture can also utilize JCET's advanced packaging production line, located nearby. For SMIC, the joint venture with JCET will facilitate ramping up of its 28-nanometer mass production. For China's IC design industry, this emerging 28-nanometer supply chain will shorten the overall manufacturing cycle time.

The 8-inch foundry cluster, focused on HHGrace

HHGrace (incorporated through the merger of Shanghai Huahong NEC Electronics Company and Grace Semiconductor Manufacturing Corporation) produces 8-inch, pure-play foundry services covering technology solutions from 1.0-micrometer[172] to 90-nanometer process nodes, focusing on advanced and differentiated technologies—including eNVM (embedded non-volatile memory), power management IC, power discrete, RF (radio-frequency electronics), and CMOS image sensors, as well as standard logic and mixed-signal sensors.

With three 8-inch wafer-fabrication facilities in Shanghai, HHGrace offers production capacity of over 124,000 8-inch wafers per month. HHGrace is also seeking to upgrade its capacity to provide foundry solutions for MEMS (microelectromechanical systems) solutions through a strategic partnership with Shanghai Quality Sensor Technology Corporation ("QST"), a Chinese company producing high-end magnetic sensors and MEMS sensors.[173] As SMIC is also diversifying into the MEMS market niche, there is reason to be concerned about a lurching threat of overcapacity.

4. CHANGES IN THE IC FOUNDRY INDUSTRY LANDSCAPE

Whether China might succeed in its trailing-node strategy depends on the impact of significant recent changes in the IC foundry industry landscape. It is an open question at this stage how the new global foundry landscape might affect China's efforts to upgrade its semiconductor industry. It is unclear, in particular, whether the emerging new global foundry landscape will create new entry possibilities for SMIC and other Chinese foundries.

Apple Acts as a Catalyst

As is so often the case in this industry, Apple acted as a catalyst for change. In response to acrimonious and unresolved patent wars, Apple switched from Samsung to TSMC as the sole supplier of Apple's next-generation application processors. As a result, the global foundry landscape is changing beyond recognition.

For a while, it looked like Apple would be TSMC's only relevant customer for 20-nanometer processors, providing it with quite some bargaining power as a *monopsonist*. As long as TSMC remains the only meaningful foundry supplier of 20-nanometer process technology, this would imply that prices for 20-nanometer foundry services would be negotiated between a *monopsonist* (Apple) and a *monopolist* (TSMC).

If such a market structure prevails, Chinese IC design firms would find it quite difficult to gain access to TSMC foundry services. As lower-tier customers, Chinese IC design firms are likely to be charged higher prices. But higher chip fabrication cost is arguably not the main concern. The main barrier to using TSMC's foundry capacity is what the industry calls MOQ, or minimum order quantity. Chinese IC design firms clearly are vastly disadvantaged relative to Apple, and may well end up having to wait for a long time to get their chips fabricated ("taped-out" in industry parlance).

In early 2014, it became clear that Chinese IC design firms were unlikely to have secure access to TSMC's foundry services. TSMC announced that its production capacity was almost fully booked for the fourth quarter of 2014. TSMC's nearly sold-out wafer production has placed most IC design houses in a dilemma as to whether they should queue up at TSMC for capacity. Since lead times for wafers usually extend to four to six months during peak business cycles, IC design houses may receive deliveries only in the first half of 2015 for wafer orders placed in the fourth quarter of 2014. Hence, Chinese IC design companies would suffer, given that time-to-market is of critical importance for success.

As timely and cost-effective access to TSMC's capacity will become even more difficult, this would in principle provide new opportunities for SMIC and other Chinese foundries to gain business from Chinese IC design companies, provided that SMIC will succeed in accelerating its upgrading to 28-nanometer process technologies. On the positive side, there are indications that SMIC's focus on trailing-node technologies has already pushed down prices and MOQs. This is important for Chinese IC design companies, as it may facilitate timely and cost-effective access to foundry capacity in China. Most importantly, Chinese IC design companies will have to struggle less with TSMC's demanding MOQ requirements.

Intensifying Competition in the Leading-Edge Foundry Business

In the meantime, however, Apple's "big bang" move to drop Samsung as its foundry supplier has now set in motion a chain of events that are likely to change further the global foundry landscape. But at this stage there is no way to predict possible outcomes. Nor is it possible to anticipate how all of this will affect China's efforts to upgrade its foundry industry.

For Samsung, the loss of Apple's foundry contracts is a massive setback. But Samsung is fighting back, and the company now seeks to compete head on with TSMC in the pure-play global foundry business for leading-edge integrated circuits. Foundry work remains an important segment for Samsung, and the company has announced an investment of $14.7 billion into a new, cutting-edge wafer fab that will use leading-edge wafer size and process technologies in order to attract foundry contracts from IC design companies.[174]

Samsung now has become the fourth-largest IC foundry, behind TSMC, Global Foundries, and UMC.[175] In 2013, Samsung had a 15 percent increase in its foundry sales and was less than $10 million behind the third-largest IC foundry in the world—UMC. According to *IC Insights*, "Samsung has the ability (i.e., leading-edge capacity and a huge capital spending budget) and desire to become a major force in the IC foundry business. It is estimated that the company's dedicated IC foundry capacity reached 150,000 300-millimeter wafers per month in the fourth quarter of 2013. Using an average-revenue-per-wafer figure of $3,000, it is estimated that Samsung's IC foundry business segment has the potential to produce annual sales of about $5.4 billion."[176]

Another potentially transformative event is IBM's decision to get rid of its semiconductor fabrication. Since the beginning of 2014, there was intense speculation about who would acquire IBM's semiconductor assets. For some observers, it seemed "…quite logical that a sale of IBM's chip manufacturing would be to China."[177] In the end, IBM's foundry operations were transferred to Global Foundries, as announced on October 21, 2014.[178] In a quite unusual arrangement, IBM pays Global Foundries $1.5 billion simply to get rid of its unprofitable chip manufacturing business. In a statement, IBM seeks to justify this embarrassing retreat, stating that the move would save it billions of dollars the company would otherwise have to spend to keep upgrading its facilities for the next generation of chip technology.[179]

The deal involves two IBM fabs: (a) East Fishkill, New York, with a 15,000-wafers-per-month capacity, which has just ramped up the 22-nanometer process used to make IBM's Power 8 processors and where 14-nanometer technology is under development; and (b) Burlington, Vermont, with a 45,000-wafers-per-month capacity—a specialty fab for analog devices, much of it for the defense industry.

There are still considerable regulatory hurdles, not only because of the defense-related products, but also because Global Foundries is primarily owned by the government of Abu Dhabi, and hence requires approval of the deal by the Committee on Foreign Investment in the United States (CFIUS). But if the deal goes through, it would not only expand Global Foundries' capacity by more than 10 percent, but it also would add more than 10,000 IBM semiconductor patents. IBM, after all, has been one of the founding fathers of semiconductor technology. IBM's semiconductor patent portfolio will thus be quite valuable, especially those patents that cover IBM's 22-nanometer and especially its 14-nanometer technologies.

It is unclear to what degree the IBM–Global Foundries deal will affect China's plans to upgrade its semiconductor foundry industry. Taiwan's UMC most likely will be negatively affected. In light of the earlier speculations that China might be the recipient of IBM's foundry assets, it is worthwhile asking: Why did China not acquire the IBM semiconductor business? Were there US national security considerations involved? Or were there doubts as to whether SMIC would have the level of competency needed for ongoing support of IBM's main line of business?

Another important player in this transformation of the global foundry landscape is Intel. By establishing its own rapidly growing Custom Foundry Group, Intel demonstrated that it intends to play an active role at the top end of the global foundry industry. Intel is actively recruiting worldwide for top foundry service specialists. With locations in the United States, Canada, and India, Intel's strategy is to provide "select customers strategic access to our leading-edge process technology and manufacturing services…[as well as] turnkey services…[such as] ASIC design services, specialty IP, wafer manufacturing, packaging, and testing." [180] A first step was a 12-year agreement, signed in February 2013, with Altera, a leading US fabless chip design company.[181] In addition, Intel is expected to add two Chinese IC design companies (Rockchip and Spreadtrum) as foundry customers.[182]

In the end, intensifying competition in the global foundry business is all driven by wafer price negotiations—and all the leading fabless companies are searching for ways to escape the high prices charged by TSMC.

From China's perspective, what matters is that the industry clearly is in turmoil due to intensifying competition among a small band of foundries that are able to offer high-volume, leading-edge foundry production over the next five years. This leading group of foundries includes TSMC, Global Foundries, UMC, Samsung, and Intel, but China's SMIC is not part of this exclusive club. These five leading-edge technology foundry leaders are fierce competitors—their main goal is to put pressure on TSMC to reduce its foundry service prices for leading-edge semiconductors. In fact, it is now expected that pricing will likely come under pressure, and that this may even be the case for leading-edge devices.

As a result, a recent forecast of growth patterns in foundry sales expects the 2014 leading-edge 28-nanometer-and-below foundry market to be about $5.1 billion, a 72 percent increase in size as compared to 2013.[183] The report concludes: "Not only is the vast majority of pure-play foundry growth coming from leading-edge production, most of the profits that will be realized come from the finer feature sizes as well."

For China, one possible impact of the emerging new global foundry landscape may well be to reduce the scope of its trailing-node upgrading strategy. In the end, it is unclear at this stage whether the emerging global foundry landscape will support China's upgrading efforts in this industry, and how all of this will affect China's new push in semiconductors. This provides yet another example of the deeply entrenched uncertainty that characterizes the dynamics of semiconductor industry development. In order to forge ahead through innovation in semiconductors, there is no doubt that China needs to experiment with a bottom-up and progressively more market-led approach to industrial policy.

5. A NEW INTEREST IN STRATEGIC PARTNERSHIPS AND MERGERS AND ACQUISITIONS

As described in Part Two of the study, strategic partnerships, joint ventures, and mergers and acquisitions (M&A) are important ingredients of China's new policy on semiconductors. Two objectives are driving these efforts: On the one hand, M&A among domestic firms are expected to create new opportunities for economies of scale and scope, and for creating synergies among firms with different specialization patterns and capabilities. A second objective is to gain access to cutting-edge technology and best-practice management techniques through strategic partnerships and joint ventures with leading global semiconductor firms.

Domestic M&A: Spreadtrum and RDA

On July 19, 2014, Tsinghua Unigroup announced that it was arranging for a merger between Spreadtrum and RDA.[184] Concluded in July 2014, the main goal of this acquisition is to create a credible competitor in the IC design market for low-end budget smartphones, not only against Taiwan's MediaTek, but also against the emerging challenge from Qualcomm.[185] Since 51 percent of Tsinghua Unigroup is owned by Tsinghua Holdings, a 100-percent state-owned limited liability corporation funded by Tsinghua University, the Spreadtrum-RDA merger is expected to deliver a new, state-owned, consolidated entity that might be able to generate sufficient economies of scale and scope.

On paper at least, the merger between Spreadtrum and RDA offers significant potential synergies. As one Chinese semiconductor industry observer explained, "Spreadtrum is weak in everything except TD-SCDMA, while RDA is strong in RF. Both are weak in application processors....Spreadtrum's integrated circuit R&D is weak, but ... [the company is] strong in software. Meanwhile, RDA is very strong in IC R&D, but has no real software development." [186]

A similar assessment is offered by a US-based industry observer: "If you wanted to create a China-based company that could (with a lot of work and a lot of money) someday rival Qualcomm, Spreadtrum and RDA are the two companies that I would pick."[187] Whether this merger will work, however, remains an open question. Both companies started out with very different business models.[188]

RDA is proud of its local roots, initially providing low-cost RF (radio frequency) circuits, especially to Chinese Shanzhai handset vendors. RDA's strategy relies on access to cheap, well-trained local engineering talent for chip design. These engineers have graduated from Chinese universities, and RDA willingly takes on the task of providing them with real-world design experience. Through intensive use of domestic engineering talent, RDA engages in exceptionally rapid cycles of prototyping and new product development. RDA chips don't need leading-edge process technology, and hence can rely on foundries with older technology. This low-key and pragmatic business model has allowed for rapid catch-up in capabilities and a sustained growth in market share at the low end of the market.

Spreadtrum, on the other hand, followed the path initially blazed by Taiwan's MediaTek, providing a turnkey platform that combines baseband and RF chips, along with the relevant associated software solutions. Leo Li, chairman, CEO, and president of Spreadtrum Communications, Inc., has more than 23 years of experience in the wireless communications industry, and has worked for Broadcom, Rockwell Semiconductors, and Ericcson. Since Li joined Spreadtrum in May 2008, the company has followed a remarkable strategy of technology leapfrogging into trailing-node process technology. This strategy has enabled it to offer feature-rich phones and move rapidly into low-end smartphones. A key milestone came in October 2010, when Spreadtrum engineers successfully prototyped a 2.5G integrated chip solution using 40-nanometer process technology, which provided the basis for a 95 percent increase in sales in 2011.

Spreadtrum's focus on trailing-node process technology culminated on June 23, 2014, with the introduction of a quad-core smartphone platform (the "SC883XG") designed with advanced 28-nanometer process technology, which integrates diverse third-generation mobile telecommunications standards, including China's TD-SCDMA standard.[189] Spreadtrum's adoption of more advanced semiconductor process technology delivers higher performance and lower power consumption, providing handset makers with a cost-effective solution for mid- to high-end handset models.

Forcing together two companies with very different cultures has triggered raw emotions and turmoil among RDA employees, who object to it. RDA's chairman and CEO, Vincent Tai, who reportedly resisted the Tsinghua Unigroup's acquisition plan, was fired by the RDA board in late 2013.[190] This apparently has created some bad blood in the company. It remains to be seen whether Spreadtrum's current commercial success as a new, combined organization will, over time, help to heal those scars.

Global Partnerships and M&A

China's efforts to realize partnerships and M&A with leading global semiconductor firms are facilitated by a tsunami of M&A deals in the global semiconductor industry. During the first half of 2015, the value of M&A deals surged to $72.6 billion, up from $16.9 billion over the whole year of 2014 (see figure 3).[191]

Figure 3. Value of Semiconductor Industry M&A Agreements Surges

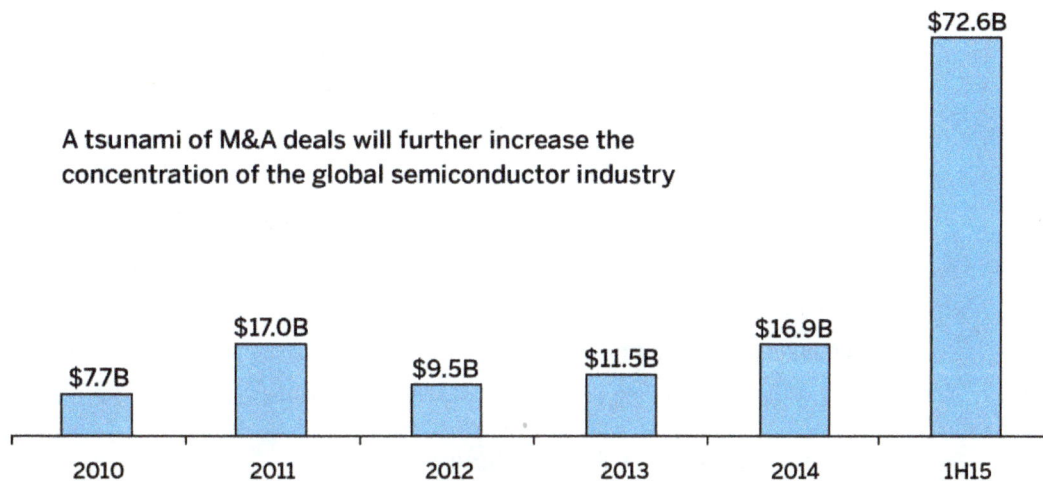

A tsunami of M&A deals will further increase the concentration of the global semiconductor industry

Source: IC Insights.

Three Major Deals Dominate Thus Far in 2015

- NXP (a spin-off of Philips) announced an agreement in March to buy Freescale (a spin-off of Motorola) for $11.8 billion in cash and stock.[192]

- In late May, Avago announced a deal to acquire Broadcom for about $37 billion in cash and stock.[193]

- On June 1, Intel reported it had struck an agreement to buy Altera[194] for $16.7 billion in cash.[195]

This rush into M&A deals is driven by the rising cost of moving to leading-edge multicomponent semiconductors (MCOs) and process technologies. As a result, the semiconductor industry is experiencing a growing pressure to consolidate size and market power through partnerships and M&A.[196]

It is unclear how the tsunami of M&A will affect China's efforts to forge ahead in the semiconductor industry. On the one hand, the proliferation of major M&A deals will further increase the concentration of the global semiconductor industry, and hence may increase barriers to entry for latecomers like China. According to *IC Insights,* "2015 has become a perfect storm for acquisitions, mergers, and consolidation among major suppliers, which are seeing sales slow in their existing market segments and need to broaden their businesses to stay in favor with investors....The increasing number of mergers and acquisitions, leading to fewer major IC manufacturers and suppliers,"[197] is increasing the concentration in the semiconductor industry.

On the other hand, the M&A tsunami seems to have simultaneously increased the interest and willingness of foreign firms to engage with Chinese firms. To some degree, this reflects a perception in the headquarters of global firms that the balance of power is shifting, providing China with greater bargaining power. China's emerging role as a lead market for mobile devices no doubt acts as a powerful magnet to global industry leaders, both in the semiconductor and in the mobile device industry, to secure long-term access to the China market. In fact, the leading global players, and especially US firms, are all now experimenting with strategic partnerships and M&A with Chinese IC design companies and foundries.[198]

In other words, China's effort to push forward with the upgrading of its semiconductor industry takes place at a time of quite dramatic changes in the global semiconductor industry. This raises two questions: Under what conditions might these global transformations facilitate China's attempt to forge ahead in semiconductors? And what adjustments in China's policies might actually be conducive for accelerating the transition to forging ahead?

China's technology planners seem to believe that, if handled correctly, the new interest by global industry leaders in strategic partnerships could create new opportunities for Chinese firms to engage in global technology sourcing.

Important examples of this new round of US-Chinese partnerships in semiconductors include, but are not restricted to, the following recently announced agreements.

Global Partnerships in the Foundry Industry

Qualcomm/SMIC
On July 2, 2014, Qualcomm and SMIC announced that they are working together on 28-nanometer wafer production for Qualcomm's latest Snapdragon processors in China.[199] Qualcomm, the leading baseband cellular processor company, states that it will offer support to accelerate the development of SMIC's 28-nanometer process technology.[200]

If Qualcomm sticks to its commitment to share critical know-how, this agreement would be a big win for SMIC. It would enable China's leading foundry to implement its trailing-node upgrading strategy, which depends on the advancement of its 28-nanometer technology.

But what is in it for Qualcomm? A combination of the following motivations may have been instrumental in Qualcomm's decision. First, the catalyst most likely has been the pressure exerted by NDRC. As Qualcomm had been singled out by the Chinese antitrust authority, appeasing the Chinese government by contracting some 28-nanometer production to SMIC might clear the air between the parties. In addition, it is also a very lucrative business.

Second, there is a general shortage of 28-nanometer production capacity, so Qualcomm may not have had much choice but to resort to second-tier production capacity available at SMIC. But SMIC is not Qualcomm's only option. On October 14, 2014, UMC announced that it has received orders from Qualcomm to produce 28-nanometer chips for fourth-generation LTE smartphones, with shipments to begin in the fourth quarter of 2014.[201] Again, this indicates how unpredictable these global transformations are, and hence how precarious key assumptions are about China's industrial upgrading scenarios for semiconductors.

Third, Qualcomm, like other leading fabless design companies, may seek to use diversification of foundry suppliers not only to get better pricing at SMIC, but also to induce price reductions by TSMC.

Fourth, as Qualcomm seeks to outmaneuver Taiwan's MediaTek and China's Spreadtrum in the low end of the smartphone market, a strategic partnership with China-based SMIC might enhance the chances to gain design-ins from Chinese smartphone vendors. This motivation has gained further urgency, as Spreadtrum has recently received a $1.5 billion investment from Intel (further discussed below).

An additional motivation for Qualcomm's decision to link up with SMIC might reflect a more fundamental shift in the semiconductor industry. As indicated earlier in this study, there is an intense debate within the industry whether the cost of producing leading-edge devices will decline and, if so, at what pace. Five industry giants—TSMC, Global Foundries, UMC, Samsung, and Intel—are betting on a speedy transition to leading-edge process technologies, starting with 20-nanometer devices. However, another equally influential group contends that barriers to such cost reductions will remain substantial for a considerable time.

Take, for instance, the respected industry figure Zvi Or-Bach,[202] who argues that "dimensional scaling beyond 28 nanometers would not provide reduction of SoC (system-on-chip) cost and, accordingly, 28 nanometers could be the preferred node for many years."[203] The Global Semiconductor Alliance (GSA), in fact, has established a 3D-IC Packaging Working Group, reflecting the importance of this potentially disruptive move towards 3D-IC based on 28-nanometer process technology.[204]

Qualcomm apparently has decided to support this approach. At the 2014 Design Automation Conference (DAC), Qualcomm declared: "One of the biggest problems is cost. We are very cost sensitive. Moore 's Law has been great. Now, although we are still scaling down, it's not cost-economic anymore. It's creating a big problem for us."[205]

In other words, Qualcomm needs to find production partners for monolithic 3D chips. As TSMC is not taking the lead in 3D chips, Qualcomm may bet that SMIC, after establishing a good relationship with Qualcomm in 28-nanometer process technology, will continue to upgrade its foundry capacities into monolithic 3D chips. According to SMIC's website, "SMIC will also extend its technology offerings on 3DIC and RF front-end wafer manufacturing in support of Qualcomm as its Snapdragon product portfolio continues to expand."[206] Or-Bach argues that, while SMIC lags behind TSMC in leading-edge nodes, this does not disqualify SMIC from using the Qualcomm deal to develop a strong position in 28-nanometer technology. If it is true that the value of the more advanced nodes is diminishing, then the SMIC-Qualcomm deal might suggest that "SMIC is positioning itself to lead in the next-generation technology driver—monolithic 3D—using the most effective node for years to come. If the rest of the foundries will ignore it, they may find themselves trailing behind SMIC in a few years, in what by then could become THE technology driver."[207]

This trend toward involving SMIC in global partnerships seems to continue. In June 2015, SMIC forged a joint venture with Huawei, Qualcomm, and the IMEC Research Institute in Louvain, Belgium, to develop its own technology for making 14-nanometer chips.[208] SMIC Advanced Technology R&D intends to have its 14-nanometer process in production by 2020. This will be a major leap forward for chip manufacturing capability in China.[209]

Global partnerships through M&A and joint ventures have also been increasing in China's semiconductor and assembly industry. Important examples include:[210]

- In May 2013, ASE acquired Toshiba's Wuxi plant (US$11 million).[211]

- In December 2013, Texas Instruments (TI) acquired the UTAC facility in Chengdu.[212]

- In June 2014, Siliconware started the third phase for its facility in Suzhou, and will add advanced packaging there.[213]

- In April 2014, Nepes, a Korean supplier of wafer bumping services, signed an agreement for a wafer-package joint venture in Huai'an, Jiangsu Province.

- In August 2014, SMIC and JCET established a joint venture in Jiangyin to set up a 12-inch wafer bumping and circuit probe testing production line.[214]

- In September 2014, Wafer Level CSP Co., Ltd, a leading Chinese supplier of semiconductor assembly services, merged with Gerad Suzhou.

- Then, in November 2014, three mergers occurred: TI announced the opening of a 300-millimeter wafer bumping facility in Chengdu, JCET announced the acquisition of Stats Chippac ($780 million), and Huatian acquired FlipChip International ($42 million).[215]

Global Partnerships in IC Design

Global partnerships and M&A also are gathering momentum in China's IC design industry. Among partnerships initiated by US firms, of particular interest are Intel's investments in two Chinese fabless companies, Rockchip (for tablet ICs) and Spreadtrum (for smartphone ICs).

Intel/Rockchip

In May 2014, Intel announced that it has entered a strategic agreement with Fuzhou Rockchip Electronics Co., a Chinese fabless IC design company focused on Android tablets,[216] to accelerate and expand the portfolio of Intel-based solutions for tablets.

This deal had well-calculated commercial and technological features. For Intel, it could certainly accelerate time to market for its tablet-related processors. There may also be a substantial public relations component, as Intel can now make the claim, "we have a Chinese partner."

A unique feature of the Android tablet market is that China-based IC design houses like Rockchip, Allwinner Technology, and Actions Semiconductor have become the main suppliers of tablet chips. The reason for this is not technological superiority, but the simple fact that leading international smartphone chip design companies have neglected this market. For them, the tablet chip market was unattractive because global demand for tablets is only about one-fifth of the smartphone market, and prices for tablet chips are only about one-third of those for smartphone chips.[217]

The success of Chinese tablet chip designers has been a wake-up call for companies like Intel, which aimed to ship 25 million tablet processors in the second half of 2014.[218] For Intel, the link with Rockchip is expected to provide it with Rockchip's ecosystem in China, including its software support and existing back-end component and market channel relationships.[219] An important motivation for Rockchip, apparently, is the intensifying competition between tablet chip design based on ARM processors, which has caused Rockchip's profits to fall and narrowed its options to differentiate itself from competing design houses.

In short, the Intel-Rockchip partnership may well have positive effects on the upgrading of China's IC design industry, provided, of course, that both companies find ways to establish effective mechanisms for technology transfer and absorption.

Intel/Spreadtrum

On September 24, 2014, Intel announced that it will pay $1.5 billion for a 20 percent stake in two Chinese mobile IC design companies (Spreadtrum Communications and RDA Microelectronics) through a deal with Tsinghua Unigroup, the government-affiliated private equity firm that owns the two mobile chipmakers. This deal is quite complex, and many essential data points have not yet been made public. For instance, how much of the $1.5 billion was paid in cash? What are the contractual arrangements for sharing intellectual property? And does this involve an IC fabrication deal for Intel's Custom Foundry Group?

In principle, this deal could provide a boost to China's efforts to upgrade its IC design industry. If RDA and Spreadtrum were able to absorb Intel's technology, this deal could empower these two companies to compete head on against Qualcomm and Taiwan's MediaTek. At the same time, Chinese smartphone vendors might also benefit, as they now would have an alternative to costly Qualcomm chipsets.

As for Intel's motivations, the company's website states that "[t]he purpose of the agreements is to expand the product offerings and adoption of Intel-based mobile devices in China and worldwide."[220] Since a new CEO took over at Intel in 2013, the company has pursued an array of deals and strategies to ensure its chip technology gets into more smartphones and tablets. Reflecting Brian Krzanich's background in semiconductor fabrication, Intel "has opened the chipmaker's prized, cutting-edge factories to paying customers."[221]

But apart from access to the thriving China market, Intel's main motivation clearly is to overcome its persistent weakness in the smartphone chip industry, which is being dominated by ARM, Qualcomm, and MediaTek. As Intel's design philosophy is shaped by the needs of the PC market, it neglected the alternative design approach of the mobile IC design industry, which is based on system-on-chip design.[222] Intel now seems to recognize that it could benefit from partnering with Spreadtrum and RDA. After all, these two Chinese companies learned early on to sell an integrated device template to smartphone vendors, who in turn have benefited through lower production costs and faster turnaround times.

By the same token, the partnership with Intel could help both Spreadtrum and RDA to reduce their dependence on ARM processors. As long as they remain "me-too" ARM IC designers, their profit margins will be limited, as ARM captures the largest share of the value added. According to industry observers, "[w]ith Intel's architecture and tech support...[Spreadtrum and RDA] will jump to the forefront and give Qualcomm, MediaTek, and [other apps processor companies] a serious run for the money."[223]

Finally, partnering with two leading Chinese mobile IC design companies could also provide Intel with new customers for its Custom Foundry Group. At this stage, this is mere speculation, as the Intel–Tsinghua Unigroup agreement does not provide much detail. Intel's 300-millimeter wafer fabrication line in Dalian, which was opened with great fanfare in 2010 to produce 65-nanometer chipsets for PCs and servers, is significantly underutilized. This by itself would provide a powerful motivation for Intel to include foundry services in the agreement with Tsinghua Unigroup.

Mergers and Acquisitions Initiated from the Chinese Side

Acquisition of OmniVison Technologies

In August 2014, US camera sensor-maker OmniVision Technologies, a leading developer of advanced digital imaging solutions, received a take-over bid from Hua Capital Management Co., Ltd (HCM), a Beijing-based investment management company.[224] As indicated in **Part Two** of the study, HCM was chosen in June to manage the sub-fund for chip design and testing under the Beijing government's $30-billion-yuan (HK$37.8 billion) Semiconductor Industry Development Fund. In response to HCM's take-over bid, OmniVision's stock price climbed by 14 percent to just over $28. The company's board of directors said it was evaluating HCM's proposal. And on September 19, 2014, HCM hired Bank of America to provide funding for its US$1.7 billion bid for US camera sensor-maker OmniVision Technologies.[225]

The proposed acquisition of OmniVision is the first example of how China's **Guidelines** are being used to acquire a foreign company, with the intention of "making that company Chinese." In fact, OmniVision has strong Chinese roots, hence the chances of success are considerable. OmniVision was co-founded by Hong Xiaoying, a Chinese immigrant and current chief executive, and the company has Chinese and Taiwanese managers among its senior ranks. In 2014, the company had sales of US$1.45 billion, but has hardly grown since 2013. However, it has attractive technology with a wide range of applications, such as cars, mobile devices, and security equipment. In 2012, OmniVision was in second place among the top-three vendors of CMOS image sensors, a group that comprised Sony, OmniVision, and Samsung, with 21 percent, 19 percent, and 18 percent, respectively, of the $6.9 billion market. OmniVision has supplied Apple with back-side illuminated CMOS image sensors for its iPhone and has a design center and testing facility in Shanghai.

On April 30, 2015, OmniVision announced that it has entered into a definitive agreement to be acquired by a consortium composed of Hua Capital Management Co., Ltd (Hua Capital), CITIC Capital Holdings Limited (CITIC Capital), and GoldStone Investment Co., Ltd. (GoldStone Investment)—collectively, the "Consortium."[226] Observers believe that this could give a significant boost to China's plans to upgrade its IC design industry. The deal also would seem to address some of the leadership's security concerns. It is, of course, an open question whether this deal will receive regulatory approval in the United States—from CFIUS and other relevant agencies—as the deal may well raise national security concerns.[227] According to USITO, the OmniVision deal may be less significant technologically, but it may well be an early herald of bigger, more substantial foreign acquisitions down the road.[228]

According to a *Wall Street Journal* report on July 14, China's Tsinghua Unigroup was planning to spend US$23 billion (or US$21 per share) to acquire US-based Micron Technology. The amount is higher than the size of the China government's China National Semiconductor Industry Investment Funds of

CNY120 billion (US$19.32 billion).[229] However, the chances for completion of this acquisition are slim. Micron is the only vendor left that produces leading-edge memories in the United States. In addition, Micron works on core semiconductors needed for High Performance Computers (HPC) and for defense applications, so-called hybrid memory cubes (HMC) for burst buffering in HPC systems. As a result, the deal will still need to pass many obstacles such as Micron's board and US government regulations, especially through the Committee on Foreign Investment in the United States (CFIUS).

China's Growing Role in Semiconductor Mergers and Acquisitions

The Thomson Reuters database on mergers and acquisitions (M&A) in the semiconductor machinery industry, as well as the semiconductor and related device manufacturing industry (NAICS codes 333295 and 334413), provides some proxy indicators of China's growing role in semiconductor mergers and acquisitions.[230] The aforementioned illustrative examples, thus, may well be quite representative.

First, M&A deals in which Chinese firms were targets display a rising trend. Out of 225 such M&A deals between January 1, 2005, and September 30, 2014, almost 30 percent (65 deals) occurred in 2013 and the first nine months of 2014. Of those 225 M&A deals, 72 percent (161 deals) were transactions where Chinese firms were both the target and the acquirer.[231]

Second, China's importance as an acquiring nation is on the rise. Of the 196 deals that involved China as the acquiring nation and that took place between 2005 and the end of September 2014, 30 percent (59 deals) were closed in 2013 and the first nine months of 2014.

China also has gained in importance both as an acquirer nation and as a target nation in the semiconductor industry. As an acquirer nation, China now is ranked fourth (with 198 deals), after the dominant United States (901 deals), South Korea (402), and Japan (231). And as a target for semiconductor M&A, China is now number three (with 227 deals), following the leading United States (847 deals) and South Korea (416), but ahead of Japan (210 deals).

Further research is needed to deepen the analysis to include detailed case studies of deals, focusing especially on the role of top acquirers (for semiconductor firms, as well as investor groups and government agencies). Of equal importance will be case studies of the role of Chinese firms, both as acquirers and as acquisition targets, and the impact of these deals on technology transfer, as well as the development of absorptive capacity and innovation capabilities of the companies involved in these deals.

China Is a Latecomer to the Current M&A Wave

On June 24, 2014, it was reported that the Chinese government was planning to take over Broadcomm's mobile baseband unit.[232] These rumors, however, were put to silence when Avago, a leading global IC design company co-headquartered in Singapore and San Jose, California, acquired Broadcomm in late May 2015.[233]

It is unclear why China's government has not proceeded to acquire Broadcom's mobile baseband unit. Many explanations are circulating in the investment community, highlighting possible constraints in terms of timing, sharing of intellectual property, and lack of trust.

There is no doubt, however, that the well-managed strategic acquisition of foreign IC design houses could help to address important weaknesses (there are aplenty!) of China's still precariously weak IC design industry. And even if strategic acquisitions would face regulatory hurdles in the United States, there are arguably other opportunities for China to implement global knowledge-sourcing strategies. For instance, former Nokia teams in Finland and around the world (including in China) could be used as sources of critically important intangible knowledge. The same may be true for engineers and engineering teams from the former Research in Motion/BlackBerry, the downsized IC division of Infineon, and other such once-important global companies.

China also may want to consider other opportunities, such as cooperating with leading centers of excellence like IMEC Research Institute in Belgium, the Delft University of Technology and the Holst Center in the Netherlands, and other centers of excellence in the Nordic countries.

In the end, China's push to upgrade its IC design industry through M&A raises, of course, a fundamental question: Does China have the managers who could make these extremely demanding acquisitions and cooperation agreements work? And, are management approaches in place that could cope with the negative side effects of internationalizing the work force of Chinese IC design companies, such as the substantial gaps in remuneration between domestic and foreign engineers and managers?

6. HOW WILL CHINA'S PUSH IN SEMICONDUCTORS AFFECT ITS EXPORTS OF ELECTRONIC FINAL PRODUCTS?

An important challenge for China's upgrading push in semiconductors is the possible impact on exports of China's electronics final products. Unfortunately, there is little discussion of this critical issue in the publicly available Chinese policy documents.

China's exports of electronic final products are of huge value and central to the country's trade and development. For 2013, the UN Comtrade database reports China's ICT (information and communications technology) exports—not including IT services and software—as $599.7 billion, which is roughly 27 percent of China's total goods exports.[234] In other words, almost a third of China's total goods exports are ICT products that are powered by semiconductors.[235] Thus, China relies on semiconductors as an essential input of a large share of the products it exports.

As China still lacks a fully developed semiconductor industry, it depends on semiconductor imports as an enabler of its exports of electronic final products. For 2013, again according to UN Comtrade data, China's ICT exports are reported as roughly 2.3 times the value of China's 2013 semiconductor imports ($261.3 billion).

Some observers in the United States suggest that China's new push to expand and upgrade its semiconductor industry may actually undermine downstream users—for instance, China-based semiconductor-consuming producers of electronic final products—and hence may erode China's export surpluses in the ICT industry.[236] It is argued that, in the event that China-based semiconductor-consuming ICT goods vendors only had access to locally produced chips, this might severely limit the quantity, type, and quality of chips they can design into their final goods. The result might be constrained performance features of those final goods, and increased costs. If these IC-consuming companies were foreign firms, they might be motivated to move to locations outside of China, where they would have unrestricted access to all the chips they needed.

To succeed amidst global competition, semiconductor-consuming ICT goods vendors based in China would need fast and unrestricted access to all chips that are available in the global market. In this scenario, China's new semiconductor policies may only be able to change buying patterns if chips designed and fabricated in China are superior in performance and price relative to competing products. The policy conclusion drawn from this argument is that China's new policies on semiconductors can only work if they allow for "free and open markets and a level competitive playing field in all markets."[237]

Chinese technology planners view these arguments with considerable skepticism. From a Chinese perspective, these arguments neglect the needs of a country that is a latecomer to this industry. In this view, China first needs to develop gradually a more integrated local industrial value chain and firm-level capabilities before it can fully reap the benefits of a more open, more transparent, and less discriminatory market for semiconductors. Chinese technology planners acknowledge that, in the short run, global technology sourcing (through imports of semiconductors, and also through joint ventures, strategic partnerships, or M&A) is necessary to accelerate catching up. They seem to be convinced, however, that forging ahead would require the development of a domestic semiconductor industry value chain, as well as relevant technology and management capabilities of Chinese firms.

To implement such a strategy, however, would require a much better understanding of how China's semiconductor industry would need to interact with its downstream, semiconductor-consuming industries. Moving to self-sufficiency in semiconductors not only is unnecessary, but it also simply would not work. It would defeat its purpose, as self-sufficiency would undermine the competitiveness of downstream, semiconductor-consuming industries. For China's new policy on semiconductors to succeed, planners and policymakers need to step back and explore possible unintended negative consequences for downstream user industries.

Thus far there has been little research on possible impacts of China's new semiconductor policy on downstream user industries. China needs in-depth empirical research on how to balance the needs of the semiconductor industry and its user industries. The only way to collect the necessary information is to move toward a bottom-up, market-led approach to "industrial policy," and to improve interaction between the government and private firms through multilevel industrial dialogues and public-private partnerships. In order to do justice to the conflicting needs of stakeholders across China's industrial value chain, China clearly needs a substantially enhanced capacity for flexible policy implementation.

Conclusions and Policy Implications

1. KEY FINDINGS

To assess the findings of this study, it is useful to highlight that policies to develop the semiconductor industry in China have experienced many changes over a relatively short period of time. In the broad scheme of things, a progressive integration into international trade and global networks of production and innovation has transformed the industry, with private firms emerging as major sources of growth, pricing decisions, and investment allocation.

In response to these transformations, China's policies had to adjust, as they began experimenting with the building blocks of a more bottom-up approach to industrial policy. At the same time, however, China's policies to develop the semiconductor industry still carry the legacy burden of the old top-down policy approaches.

Compared to the past, what makes the new policy more aligned with market principles? The study shows that the new policy resorts to investment rather than subsidy as the tool of industrial policy. The government participates in equity investment and claims it will do so without intervening in management decisions. In essence, this policy is expected to reduce the cost of funds for a selected group of firms, which is to form a "national team" in the semiconductor industry. Lower costs of funds will induce more investments in capacity and R&D. It is expected that this approach to investment funding will accelerate the transition from catching up to forging ahead through innovation. With equity ownership, the government believes that it can better monitor the performance of the firms than in the case of subsidy. If the firms do not perform, the government can replace the management teams.

It remains unclear, however, how this approach is different from the case of state-owned enterprises, where the government can also monitor and replace the management. Another open question for further research is whether it really makes a difference that Spreadtrum and RDA are governed by managers at Tsinghua University Fund rather than the Beijing government. A related unresolved puzzle is how private equity fund managers, who are supposed to maximize the return on capital, can nevertheless serve as a proxy for the government and support its policy to strengthen indigenous innovation.

This study documents that China's new policy to upgrade its semiconductor industry through innovation, as described in the **Guidelines to Promote National Integrated Circuit Industry Development**, does not represent a radical break with a deeply embedded statist tradition. Rather, it retains many aspects of the "old industrial policy" doctrine, placing final control over whatever changes might occur in the hands of the government and, in the final instance, the top leadership.

Within these boundaries, however, the study detects important changes in the direction of a bottom-up, market-led approach to industrial policy. The study highlights a shift in the composition and governance of the **IC Industry Support Small Leading Group**. It is now more common to have experts play an active role in policy formulation and implementation, especially those who have intimate knowledge both of the international industry and the national policy circles.

Equally important are potentially quite important shifts in the allocation of investments funds. A closer look at the **Beijing IC Industry Equity Investment Fund** finds that the use of professional investment fund managers, as opposed to government subsidies or investment, signals a new approach to industrial policy that focuses on building a strong and sustainable investment environment in China. This does not imply that China's approach to investment funding will converge any time soon with a US-style model of investment finance. More likely is the development of a *hybrid* model, one that seeks to combine the logic of equity investment fund management with the objectives of China's IC development strategy. Whether this hybrid model of industrial policy will work will have to be examined in future research.

The study also highlights additional examples of at least incremental movements toward a more bottom-up, market-led approach to industrial policy. For instance, China's technology planners no longer view global transformations in markets and technology merely as threats. In this more assertive view, global transformations are seen as opportunities for China to forge ahead in semiconductors. The study has analyzed in quite some detail how China's new semiconductor strategy seeks to identify upgrading opportunities for China's semiconductor industry that could benefit from four global transformations: (a) the demand pull from mobile devices, (b) new opportunities for China's IC foundries in trailing-node semiconductor technologies, (c) changes in the IC foundry industry landscape, and (d) a new interest in strategic partnerships and mergers and acquisitions (M&A).

An important, largely unresolved challenge for China's policies on semiconductors is the possible impact on exports of China's electronics final products. Research for this study did not find much discussion of this critical issue in the publicly available Chinese policy documents. Despite movements in the right direction, is would seem fair to state that the new semiconductor strategy's capacity for flexible policy adjustments remains limited, and that multilayered industrial dialogues among key stakeholders in the industry are still at an early stage.

Finally, a defining characteristic of China's new semiconductor strategy is a persistent tension and frequent vacillation between more statist and more bottom-up industrial policies. To some degree, this reflects China's legacy of the planned economy. But given the tremendous progress that China has realized in this industry, it is time to shift the focus of attention to domestic impediments that are still constraining progress to a "new industrial policy" approach, one which, of course, would need to reflect and address the specific needs of China's evolving economy.

2. WHAT COULD DERAIL THE UPGRADING OF CHINA'S SEMICONDUCTOR INDUSTRY?

It is time now to address four issues that might well derail China's policies to upgrade its semiconductor industry. A detailed analysis is beyond the scope of this study. Instead, an attempt is made to raise some specific questions for future research.

Threat of Overcapacity
Will China's push to upgrade its semiconductor foundry industry create overcapacity, such as in the solar PV industry and wind power? As is typical for China, the implementation of the semiconductor policy is left to the local governments. As Kenneth Lieberthal demonstrates, "[t]he last three decades of

reforms…have greatly empowered the leaders…in every province, municipality, and township to act in entrepreneurial ways to grow the GDP of their locality every year."[238] Each locality is quite inward looking, and far less concerned with national issues.

This has negative consequences. Most importantly, local governments have become masters in producing overcapacity due to misaligned incentives that are focused exclusively on the region's GDP growth. In addition, local protectionist policies reduce the potential impact of scale economies and economies of scope. "Even with a very large national market, many plants produce at suboptimal scale, and many investment decisions are made on the basis of political criteria."[239]

This raises the question: Why should this be different for the semiconductor foundry industry? Some observers argue that, unlike in the solar PV industry, technological barriers and the huge minimum investment burdens may prevent overinvestment in the IC foundry industry. Future research needs to assess how realistic this argument is.

China's Fragmented Innovation System[240]

From the outside, China's innovation policy often seems to present a homogenous picture of a top-down "model of neo-mercantilist state developmental capitalism."[241] But that picture fails to capture the surprisingly fragmented Chinese innovation system that involves diverse stakeholders with conflicting interests.

There is no doubt that China's leaders are committed to indigenous innovation as the key to removing poverty and to accelerating China's catching up with the United States, the EU, and Japan. Indigenous innovation is considered essential not only for moving beyond the precarious export-oriented growth model. At stake really is the survival of the system. Chinese leaders understand that export-led growth can no longer guarantee the continued rapid expansion of the economy. Hence, they place all their bets on indigenous innovation as a catalyst for industrial upgrading.

But the implementation of this strategic vision is constrained by the fragmentation of China's innovation system, which involves diverse stakeholders with conflicting interests. By somewhat simplifying, it is possible to distinguish four main groups of stakeholders in China's innovation system.

First, China's exporting industry is a strong supporter of compliance with WTO commitments and progressive trade liberalization—for instance, as participants of the Information Technology Agreement (ITA). This position reflects China's deep integration into global corporate networks of production and innovation. Support for greater compliance with international standards also comes from leading Chinese ICT firms that have accumulated a critical mass of intellectual property rights, such as Huawei, ZTE, Lenovo, and Haier.

A *second* group of stakeholders emphasizes the need to improve China's absorptive capacity in order to benefit from foreign technology through strengthened domestic capabilities. An equally important objective is to reduce the cost of using foreign technology through patent licensing fees, and to reduce China's dependence on foreign technology. Strong support for developing China's indigenous innovation capabilities can be found in public research institutes; in SOEs in China's priority industries (such as telecommunications and semiconductors); in parts of the domestic high-tech industry that seek to take away domestic market share from multinational corporations; as well as in some minor parts of the defense and space industry. This coalition of domestic stakeholders is supporting, for instance, policies to reduce licensing fees to foreign patent holders.

A *third* group of stakeholders are "copycats" that seek to retain space for low-cost reverse engineering, unauthorized copying, and opportunistic *incremental* innovations. For quite some time, the main examples of these types of successful, low-cost innovations were no-name Shanzhai (unlicensed) handsets that, until a few years ago, accounted for around 40 percent share of the Chinese handset market. More recently, Chinese mobile device vendors like Xiaomi began practicing patent-avoiding strategies. As described earlier in the study, these companies have benefited from special provisions of Qualcomm's cross-licensing model in China, which has protected these companies from patent litigation. The main thrust of these stakeholders is to prevent a modernization of China's laws and regulations on intellectual property rights (IPR), as well as a more active implementation of China's anti-monopoly policy. The study shows that the lobbying power of this third group of stakeholders is in decline.

Fourth, a majority of stakeholders in the defense and space industry, as well as in energy-related industries such as oil and gas and "smart electricity grids," seeks to broaden the space for developing mission-oriented complex technology systems through aggressive indigenous innovation policies. For instance, these stakeholders view information security and certification regulations as a critically important policy tool in China's innovation strategy. Relevant policy initiatives include, for instance, China's National Information Assurance Policy Framework Multilevel Protection Scheme (MLPS), issued by the Ministry of Public Security in June 2007; and CNCA's Information Security Testing and Certification Regulations, which are driven by fears that China's critical information networks provide an easy target of attack, sabotage, and terrorism by hostile forces and elements. A strategic assumption is that control over standards and a strong Chinese information security industry are necessary to protect China's information security.

It is difficult for outsiders to assess which of these four stakeholder coalitions has most leverage in shaping decisions on China's innovation policies. A detailed analysis of recent developments in China's innovation policies finds a fairly consistent pattern of how China responds to foreign complaints.[242] In round one, China's government regulations make quite demanding requirements that deviate from established international norms. This typically gives rise to a wave of criticism from foreign enterprises and business organizations, but also from Chinese companies that have established a significant position in the international market and have begun to accumulate a reasonably broad portfolio of intellectual property rights. In response to this criticism, round two then leads to some adjustments in the government regulations, combining a selective relaxation of contested requirements with persistent ambiguity.

In short, fragmentation explains a major weakness of China's innovation system, i.e. potential complementarities between its diverse innovation models remain grossly underutilized. China's four innovation models largely coexist in splendid isolation, as they remain separated by conflicting interests of diverse stakeholders and intra-agency rivalries that are characteristic for China's innovation system.

Overall, however, this study shares Scott Kennedy's assessment that, when push comes to shove on how to implement China's indigenous innovation policy, "the most mercantilist elements are regularly rebuffed, and given the array of interests in favor of a more open innovation strategy, that pattern is unlikely to change….[As] Chinese companies and officials are engaging—if not fully embracing—global regimes for intellectual property, standards, and even government procurement…a socialization process is gradually encouraging more constructive behavior so that competition and cooperation occur within the context of a clearer set of boundaries." [243]

Cybersecurity

Will the leadership's cybersecurity objectives derail the industrial upgrading scenario? China's policy on information security seeks to protect China-based information systems against perceived threats to national and public security.[244] The underlying strategic rationale provides an example of Susan Shirk's description of China as a "fragile superpower."[245]

There is a widespread concern among China's leadership, especially in the military and the Ministry of Public Security (MPS), that China is exposed to nontraditional and asymmetric threats to national security. Information technology is viewed as a double-edged sword. China's resurgence both as an economic and military power challenges incumbent global and regional leaders. China's leadership believes that Western IT systems use product backdoors, system loopholes, and Trojan horses to steal China's national secrets and to slow down China's rise as a global economic power.[246]

China's leaders also fear that persistent leadership in IT provides ample opportunities for Western powers to use export controls, control over technical standards, and high licensing fees to stifle China's development and force reliance on Western technology. As a latecomer to the global race in information and communications technology, China has weak capabilities in information system management, and there is a general lack of knowledge and institutions that are capable of protecting China's critical information systems.

To counter these threats, the China State Informatization Leaders Group (SILG), a high-level Chinese leadership body was developed in 2003 as part of China's five-year national cybersecurity strategy (SILG Document 27) to address threats to information systems and networks through an indigenous national assurance system under firm domestic control. Apparently this confidential document contains a comprehensive strategy, with its priorities reaching just about every aspect of information security technology.

In response to Edward Snowden's disclosure of US National Security Agency (NSA) global surveillance practices in China and elsewhere,[247] China's concern with cybersecurity receives prominent attention in the **Guidelines to Promote National Integrated Circuit Industry Development**. The **Guidelines** argue that, in order to improve the security and reliability of ICT products and services in China, it is necessary to:

a. "Promote the wide use and government procurement of 'safe and reliable' software and hardware, including IC.

b. "Encourage telecommunications, Internet, and end-product companies to make procurement decisions based on safety and reliability of products.

c. "Form an industry standards system and develop safe and reliable capabilities in emerging industries (IoT, Big Data, cloud computing)." [248]

This raises the following questions for future research: Is the drumbeat on security used primarily as a tactic to mobilize support for aggressive investment funding?[249] Or is this focus on security an overriding concern for China's leadership that will cast aside many of the aforementioned economic considerations? How serious, in fact, are potentially short-term negative impacts? For instance, according to some observers, much of the Chinese government is in gridlock, as no one dares to start new initiatives in light of the renewed focus on security (under the guise of the anti-corruption campaign). And, longer term, what would be the fate of China's semiconductor industry if security concerns would really sideline China's commercial and industrial interests, and if China would indeed move back to creating its own self-reliant system of semiconductor and information and communications technologies?

Trade and Investment Agreements

Finally, future research would need to examine how new international and investment agreements might affect China's efforts to upgrade its semiconductor industry. A defining characteristic of today's international trading system is that megaregional trade agreements are gaining in importance relative to the gridlocked Doha Development Round of multilateral trade negotiations.[250] Examples are the WTO Government Procurement Agreement (GPA), the Information Technology Agreement (ITA), the Trans-Pacific Partnership Agreement (TPP), and the Transatlantic Trade and Investment Agreement (TTIP).

Of immediate interest is the Information Technology Agreement (ITA).[251] By reducing barriers to trade that have not been adequately addressed in multilateral negotiations, the ITA is widely expected to facilitate the diffusion of innovation in the critically important information and communications technology (ICT) industry.[252]

Proponents of ITA emphasize that developing countries, and especially emerging economies, could reap significant innovation gains from the trade agreement, as tariff reduction will lower import prices, improve market access for exporters, and enhance competition.[253] China benefited substantially from the first round of ITA trade liberalization. Since 2013, ITA members were negotiating a possible substantial expansion of the list of products covered by ITA, the so-called ITA-2 round. It took quite a while to get to an agreement, and the real sticking point remained advanced semiconductors, the so-called MCOs (multicomponent semiconductors), where China bargained hard to get an acceptable solution.

This negotiation strategy reflected China's overriding concern to upgrade its semiconductor industry through innovation and the development of generic technology platforms like sophisticated multicore semiconductors, the so-called MCOs. However, ITA-2 without China would have been an oxymoron. As documented in this study, not only is China the world's biggest smartphone market, it is also by far the most important market for US semiconductor firms. As John Neuffer, a former senior vice-president of global policy at the Information Technology Industry Council (ITIC) pointed out in November 2013, "China has got to be part of this. They are too big a player. You can't have an outcome without the Chinese."[254]

In short, a successful conclusion of ITA-2 negotiations required first and foremost an agreement between the United States and China on how to resolve the tariff treatment of MCOs. That bilateral agreement was reached in November 2014, when President Obama announced success in negotiations with China. However, that US-China agreement prompted fresh opposition from South Korea (about LCD display panels and lithium ion batteries), the EU (about analog car radios), and Taiwan (about flat-panel displays). But in the end, the expanded ITA-2 deal went through on July 27, 2015, as the United States agreed to further small concessions to China to help South Korea and the EU secure their own deals with China.[255]

This outcome shows that China needed a successful ITA-2 as much as the United States did. It also shows that in order to reach its overriding objective, China's trade negotiators know how to compromise without undermining its strategy of upgrading the semiconductor industry. China's negotiation strategy confirms that pragmatism continues to shape its trade and industrial policy in semiconductors. This supports the observation of Brandeis University's Peter Petri: "China is not averse to intervening, but it has done that against the background of a lot of liberalization. It's paying off."[256]

3. RISING UNCERTAINTY REQUIRES FLEXIBLE POLICY IMPLEMENTATION

The analysis of China's policies on semiconductors has shown that global transformations in the semiconductor industry are facilitating China's efforts to move from catching up to forging ahead in semiconductors. A second important finding, however, is the precarious nature of these opportunities— basic parameters that determine how China will fare may change at short notice and in unpredictable ways. Rising complexity of technology, business organization, and competitive dynamics are the root causes for such uncertainty.

Today, innovation in semiconductors depends increasingly on science and on interactions of multiple and very diverse stakeholders through geographically dispersed innovation networks that extend the boundaries of industries and nations.[257] For semiconductors, competition is centered on the increasingly demanding performance features for electronic systems. Whether one looks at laptops, smartphones, mobile base stations, medical equipment, or car electronics, these electronic systems all need to become lighter, thinner, shorter, smaller, faster, and cheaper, as well as having more functions and using less power. To cope with these demanding performance requirements, engineers have pushed modular design and system integration, with the result that major building blocks of a mobile handset are now integrated on a chip.

Design teams also need to cope with the accelerating pace of technical change. Essential performance features are expected to double every two years, time to market is critical, and product lifecycles are rapidly shrinking to a few months. Only those companies thrive that succeed in bringing new products to the relevant markets ahead of their competitors. Of critical importance is that a firm can build specialized capabilities quicker and at lower cost than its competitors.[258]

Arguably, the most important manifestation of rising technological complexity is the convergence of ICT infrastructures for the Internet, wireless, and mobile communications, and cloud computing that culminates in ubiquitous networks (or the Internet of Everything).[259]

The root cause for these demanding requirements for technology development is the emergence of a "winner-takes-all" competition model, described by Intel's Andy Grove.[260] In the fast-moving ICT industry, success or failure is defined by return on investment and speed to market, and every business function, including R&D and standard development, is measured by these criteria.

Intensifying technology-based competition has provoked fundamental changes in business organizations. No firm, not even a global market leader like Intel or Qualcomm, can mobilize all the diverse resources, capabilities, and repositories of knowledge internally.

Corporations have responded with a progressive modularization of all stages of the value chain and its dispersion across boundaries of firms, countries, and sectors through multilayered corporate networks of production and innovation. The complexity of these global networks is mind-boggling. According to Peter Marsh, the *Financial Times's* manufacturing editor, "[e]very day 30 million tons of materials valued at roughly $80 billion are shifted around the world in the process of creating some one billion types of finished products."[261]

While the proliferation of global production networks goes back to the late 1970s, a more recent development is the rapid expansion of global innovation networks (GINs), driven by the relentless slicing and dicing of engineering, product development, and research.[262] Empirical research documents that this has further increased the complexity of global corporate networks. GINs now involve multiple actors and firms that differ substantially in size, business model, market power, and nationality of ownership, giving rise to a variety of networking strategies and network architectures.

The flagship companies that control key resources and core technologies, and hence shape these networks, are still overwhelmingly from the United States, the European Union, and Japan. However, there are also now network flagships from emerging economies, especially from Asia. Huawei, China's leading telecommunications equipment vendor, and the second-largest vendor worldwide, provides an example of a Chinese GIN that can illustrate the considerable organizational complexity involved in such networks.[263]

In short, rising complexity and uncertainty is the defining characteristic of today's global semiconductor industry. Uncertainty implies that it is always preferable to have built-in redundancy and freedom to choose among alternatives rather than seeking to impose from the top the "one best way" of doing things.[264] First, rising complexity drastically reduces the time available for policy formulation and implementation, which makes it practically impossible to get solutions right the first time. There may have to be many policy iterations, based on trial and error, and an extended dialogue with all stakeholders to find out what works and what doesn't.

Second, rising complexity makes it difficult to predict possible outcomes of any particular policy measure, especially unexpected negative side effects, of which there is an almost endless variety. In fact, a small change in one policy variable can have far-reaching and often quite unexpected disruptive effects on many other policy variables and outcomes. To cope with this complexity challenge requires a capacity for flexible adjustments in policies meant, for instance, to strengthen the absorptive capacity and R&D investment of Chinese firms.

And, third, it is next to impossible to predict the full consequence of interactions among an increasingly diverse population of both domestic and international stakeholders in China's semiconductor industry. Given the diversity of competing stakeholders, the results of a particular industrial support policy depends much more on negotiations, gaming, and compromises than on the logical clarity and technical elegance of that policy.[265]

For China's policy to upgrade its semiconductor industry, flexible policy implementation is required to cope with this rising complexity and uncertainty. Prioritization is no longer the exclusive role of the state planner. The focus of policymaking thus needs to shift from the selection of priority sectors, technologies, and areas for public investment to the facilitation of "smart specialization," defined as "an interactive process in which the private sector is discovering and producing information about new activities and the government provides [incentives and removes regulatory constraints] for the search to happen, assesses potential, and empowers those actors most capable of realizing the potentials."[266]

Notes

[1] Deng Xiaoping, as quoted in Jon Sigurdson, *Technology and Science in the People's Republic of China: An Introduction* (Oxford: Pergamon Press, 1980), 15.

[2] T. Clissold, "How to do business without western rules," *Financial Times, August 26, 2015: 7.*

[3] T. Clissold, *Mr. China: A Memoir* (New York: Harper Collins Publishers, 2006)

[4] K. Lieberthal, *Managing the China Challenge: How to Achieve Corporate Success in the People's Republic* (Washington, DC: Brookings Institution Press, 2011), 7.

[5] Chen Datong, presentation at Global Leadership Summit, Global Semiconductor Alliance (GSA), Shanghai, http://www.gsaglobal.org/events/2014/0320/speakers.aspx#Chen.

[6] World Bank and the Development Research Center of the State Council of China, *China 2030: Building a Modern, Harmonious, and Creative Society* (Washington, DC: World Bank, 2013), http://www.worldbank.org/content/dam/Worldbank/document/China-2030-complete.pdf.

[7] Xue Lan, "Promoting Innovation-Driven Development in China and International S&T Collaboration," December 5, keynote at HKUST Business School, December 5, 2014, http://www.bm.ust.hk/~mgmt/2014MOR/Panel1/Panel1_LanXue.pdf.

[8] Liu Xielin, "Innovation Driven Development and Its Implication for Innovation and IPR," presentation at the conference New Perspectives on Innovation and Intellectual Property Policy in China: What Does the Evidence Say? May 18–19, 2015, UC San Diego, http://china.ucsd.edu/_files/np-2015/Panel%203%20-%20LIU_Xielin.pdf.

[9] For a review of key policy documents, see Zhu Xinghua, "Diagnosis of NIS and Current Comprehensive Reform for STI in China," Third Asia-Pacific NIS Forum, April 8–9, 2015, Bangkok, Thailand, http://apctt.org/pdf/China-Dr-Xinghua.pdf. Important examples include: the *8th CPC Central Committee 3rd Plenum Communiqué*, November 12, 2013, as presented and analyzed in US-China Economic and Security Review Commission; *Third Plenum Economic Reform Proposals: A Scorecard*, Staff Research Backgrounder, November 19, 2013, http://origin.www.uscc.gov/sites/default/files/Research/Backgrounder_Third%20Plenum%20Economic%20Reform%20Proposals--A%20Scorecard%20%282%29.pdf; Communist Party of China (CPC) Central Committee and the State Council, 2015, *Report on the Role of Innovation-Driven Development Amid the Economic "New Normal" of Slower Growth*, March 23, 2015, http://news.xinhuanet.com/english/2015-03/23/c_134090877.htm.

[10] As documented in M. McCuaig-Johnston and Moxi Zhang, *China Embarks on Major Changes in Science and Technology*, China Institute of Alberta, Occasional Paper Series 2, no. 2, June 2015.

[11] Liu 2015, slide 9.

[12] McCuaig-Johnston and Zhang, 2015: pages 2 and 3.

[13] For the science and technology plan, see State Council, "China's Medium- and Long-Term Plan for Science and Technology Development (2005–2020)," February 9, 2006, http://www.gov.cn/english/2006-02/09/content_184426.htm. On the SEI plan, see 国务院关于印发"十二五"国家战略性新兴产业发展规划的通知 ["The State Council Notification on the Long-term Development Plan for Strategic Emerging Industries during the 12th Five Year Plan"], 国发〔2012〕28号, July 7, 2012.

[14] For empirical evidence, see D. Ernst and B. Naughton, *Global Technology Sourcing in China's Integrated Circuit Design Industry: A Conceptual Framework and Preliminary Findings,* East-West Center Working Papers, Economics Series, no. 131, August 2012; D. Ernst, "Can Chinese IT Firms Develop Innovative Capabilities Within Global Knowledge Networks?" in *Greater China's Quest for Innovation*, eds. Marguerite Gong Hancock, Henry S. Rowen, and William F. Miller (Shorenstein Asia Pacific Research Center and Brookings Institution Press, 2008); D. Ernst and B. Naughton, "China's Emerging Industrial Economy-Insights from the IT Industry," in *China's Emergent Political Economy—Capitalism in the Dragon's Lair*, ed. C. McNally (Routledge, 2007).

[15] USITO, *Guidelines to Promote National Integrated Circuit Industry Development* (unauthorized translation of document published by the Ministry of Industry and Information Technology, the National Development and Reform Commission, the Ministry of Finance, and the Department of Science and Technology), United States Information Technology Office, Beijing, June 24, 2014.

[16] A growing literature on "new" industrial policies argues that, under conditions of uncertainty, "…[t]he right model for industrial policy is not that of an autonomous government applying…taxes or subsidies, but of strategic collaboration between the private sector and the government with the aim of uncovering where the most significant obstacles to restructuring lie and what type of interventions are most likely to remove them.…[T]he analysis of industrial policy needs to focus not on the policy outcomes—which are inherently unknowable ex ante—but on getting the policy process right." Passage from D. Rodrik, "Industrial Policy for the Twenty-First Century," Research Working Paper 04-047, John F. Kennedy School of Government, Harvard University (November 2004): 3. See also D. Foray, *Smart Specialisation: Opportunities and Challenges for Regional Innovation Policy*, (London and New York: Routledge, 2014).

[17] See, for instance, D. Ernst, "Complexity and Internationalisation of Innovation: Why Is Chip Design Moving to Asia?" *International Journal of Innovation Management* 9, no. 1, special issue in honor of Keith Pavitt (March 2005): 47–73.

[18] Classic sources include L. Kim, *Imitation to Innovation: The Dynamics of Korea's Technological Learning* (Boston: Harvard Business School Press, 1997); R.R. Nelson, *Technology, Institutions, and Economic Growth* (Cambridge: Harvard University Press, 2005). See also J.E. Stiglitz and B.C. Greenwald, *Creating a Learning Society: A New Approach to Growth, Development and Social Progress* (New York: Columbia University Press, 2014).

[19] See D. Ernst and B. Naughton, "China's Emerging Industrial Economy: Insights from the IT Industry" in *China's Emergent Political Economy: Capitalism in the Dragon's Lair*, ed. C.A. McNally (London and New York: Routledge and East-West Center Studies. 2008). China's semiconductor firm fits the pattern observed by Nick Lardy: "Private firms have become the main source of economic growth…and the major contributor to China's growing and now large role as a global trader." From N. Lardy, *Markets over Mao: The Rise of Private Business in China* (Washington, DC: Peterson Institute for International Economics, September 2014): 4.

[20]C. Antonelli, "The Systemic Dynamic of Technological Change: An Introductory Frame," in *Elgar Handbook on the System Dynamics of Technological Change* (Cheltenham, UK: Edward Elgar Publishing Ltd., 2011).

[21] This raises an important question for further research: How do private actors behave in China's regulatory and policy environment compared to their behavior in countries with largely unfettered market forces, like the US and the UK?

[22] D. Ernst, "Production and Innovation Networks, Global," in *Encyclopedia of Global Studies,* eds. H. Anheier and M. Juergensmeyer (Thousand Oaks, CA: SAGE Publications, 2012), 1393–97; D. Ernst, *A New Geography of Knowledge in the Electronics Industry? Asia's Role in Global Innovation Networks*, Policy Studies, no. 54 (Honolulu: East-West Center, 2009); D. Ernst, "Complexity and Internationalization of Innovation: Why Is Chip Design Moving to Asia?" *International Journal of Innovation Management* 9, no. 1, special Issue in honor of Keith Pavitt (March 2005): 47–73; D. Ernst and Linsu Kim, "Global Production Networks, Knowledge Diffusion and Local Capability Formation," *Research Policy* 31, no. 8/9, special issue in honor of Richard Nelson and Sydney Winter (2002): 1417–29.

[23] Liu 2015

[24] US Department of Commerce, International Trade Administration, *2015 Top Markets Report Semiconductors and Semiconductor Manufacturing Equipment: A Market Assessment Tool for US Exporters* (July 2015): 15. http://trade.gov/topmarkets/pdf/Semiconductors_Top_Markets_Report.pdf.

[25]PwC, "A Decade of Unprecedented Growth: China's Impact on the Semiconductor Industry 2014 Update," (January 2015): 11, http://www.pwc.com/en_GX/gx/technology/chinas-impact-on-semiconductor-industry/assets/china-semicon-2014.pdf; Allen Lu, "Challenges and Opportunities for China in the Semiconductor Industry," SEMI Global Update, August 4, 2015, www.semi.org.

[26] US Department of Commerce 2015: p.13.

[27] These foreign companies are either contract manufacturers (the so-called electronic manufacturing service providers), such as Taiwan's Foxconn, or global brand-name companies with China-based factories, such as Samsung. See PwC, *A Decade of Unprecedented Growth: China's Impact on the Semiconductor Industry 2014 Update*, http://www.pwc.com/gx/en/technology/chinas-impact-on-semiconductor-industry/2014-section-1.jhtml.

[28] In 2013, almost 17 percent of semiconductors consumed in China were purchased outside and trans-shipped/consigned into China for consumption (as noted in the 2014 PwC report listed above).

[29] PwC, 2015.

[30] Data are from the China Center of Information Industry Development (CCID) Consulting and the China Semiconductor Industry Association (CSIA), as quoted by PwC's Ed Pausa in an email to the author, July 6, 2014.

[31] "Fabless companies" is a widely used industry shorthand for IC design companies. These companies design ICs, but they outsource their fabrication to specialized providers of so-called IC foundry services.

[32] *IC Insights*, "China Charts New Course in Targeting Worldwide IC industry—Fablesss!" 2015, http://www.icinsights.com/news/bulletins/China-Charts-New-Course-In-Targeting-Worldwide-IC-IndustryFabless/ Nineteen US companies were represented among the top-50 fabless suppliers in 2014, and they accounted for 64 percent of the total top-50 fabless company IC sales. In 2014, Japan held less than 1 percent and the "other" countries (e.g., South Korea, Singapore, etc.) represented only 6 percent of the market held by the top-50 fabless IC suppliers.

[33] Hsiao-Wen Wang, "China's Semiconductor Grab—TSMC, MediaTek in the Bull's Eye," *CommonWealth Magazine*, August 21, 2014, http://english.cw.com.tw/article.do?action=show&id=14830.

[34] As discussed later, Spreadtrum and RDA have been merged.

[35] For instance, the combined revenues of the top-10 Chinese IC design companies of $1.57 billion is much lower than the individual results posted by each of the top-five global fabless companies (China's Fabless Profile, *EE Times Confidential Special Report 2011*). According to MIIT research, the total combined revenue of China's 500 or so IC design companies equals around 60 percent to 70 percent of the revenue of Qualcomm. (USITO, interview with Miao Wei, MIIT, Director of Department of Informatization, on the background, significance, and key points from the *Guidelines*, June 25, 2014, page 3.) According to industry sources, 223 Chinese fabless companies lost money in 2013, and many of the fabless companies have fewer than 50 people.

[36] There are signs, however, that Chinese computer scientists are working to overcome this weakness. In fact, on July 14, 2015, during a keynote at the ISC 2015 High Performance Computing Conference in Frankfurt, Prof. Yutong Lu—director of the System Software Laboratory, School of Computer Science, National University of Defense Technology, Changsha, China—announced that China will be using homegrown digital signal processors (DSPs) to reach 100 petaflops on the upgraded Chinese supercomputer Tianhe-2, which is the world's fastest. In contrast to general processors like the Godson, DSPs are designed to achieve better power efficiency, and are thus more suitable in portable devices such as mobile phones because of power-consumption constraints.

[37] *Xinhuanet*, "Chinese OS Expected to Debut in October," August 24, 2014, http://news.xinhuanet.com/english/china/2014-08/24/c_133580158.htm.

[38] Y. Yoshida, "China Launching Its Own OS, Seriously?" *EETimes*, August 25, 2014, http://www.eetimes.com/document.asp?doc_id=1323638.

[39] See Part Three for details.

[40] A. Shilov, "TSMC Builds World's First 32-Core Networking Chip Using 16nm Fin FET Process," *Kitguru*, September 25, 2014, http://www.kitguru.net/components/cpu/anton-shilov/tsmc-builds-worlds-first-32-core-networking-chip-using-16nm-finfet-process-technology/.

[41] PwC, 2015.

[42] China's successful catching up and forging ahead in semiconductor assembly, testing, and packaging supports Ken Lieberthal's important observation that prefaces the current study: "Pragmatism has been a hallmark of China's reforms over the past 30 years, as Chinese leaders have not flinched from a realistic view of their challenges. They typically experiment with various approaches before deciding on the best ways to address major concerns." Passage from K. Lieberthal, *Managing the China Challenge: How to Achieve Corporate Success in the People's Republic*, Washington, DC: Brookings Institution Press, 2011), 7.

[43] CCID and CSIA data quoted in H. Jones, "China Wants To Be No. 1," *EETimes*, August 20, 2014.

[44] Derwent Worldwide Patent data quoted in PwC, 2014.

[45] For instance, an important new study by Robin Feldman and Mark Lemley finds that the impact of patent licensing on innovation is dismal, even when the licensing requests or lawsuits came from product-producing companies and from universities rather than from patent trolls. The authors conclude that their findings "…suggest that licensing from patent demands is not serving much of an innovation promotion function at all—no matter what type of party initiates the licensing demand."(Passage from Robin Feldman and Mark A. Lemley, "Does Patent Licensing Mean Innovation?" February 15, 2015, available at SSRN: http://ssrn.com/abstract=2565292.)

[46] MCOs are used in a wide variety of products, including smartphones, tablets, medical devices, household appliances, and car parts such as braking, steering, and air bag systems. MCOs thus can be classified under a wide range of trade classification subheadings. As a result, no one really knows for sure how important MCOs are for US exports. USITC estimates that in 2011, sales of MCOs accounted for between 1.5 and 3 percent of global semiconductor sales, or an estimated $1.2 to $2.4 billion. (USITC. 2013. *The Information Technology Agreement, Advice and Information on the Proposed Expansion*, Part 2: p. VI.) http://www.usitc.gov/publications/332/pub4382.pdf.

[47] National Research Council, *The New Global Ecosystem in Advanced Computing: Implications for U.S. Competitiveness and National Security* (Washington: DC: The National Academies Press, 2012).

[48] For details on China's position in ITA, see D. Ernst, *The Information Technology Agreement, Industrial Development and Innovation—India's and China's Diverse Experiences* (Geneva: The World Economic Forum and the International Center for Trade and Sustainable Development/ICTSD, 2014), http://e15initiative.org/wp-content/uploads/2014/11/E15_Innovation_Ernst_FINAL.pdf.

[49] Limin He, corporate vice president of Cadence, a leading provider of computer-aided IC design tools, as quoted in "China Fabless Semiconductor Panel: Don't Pack Your Bags Just Yet," http://community.cadence.com/cadence_blogs_8/b/ii/archive/2014/06/18/china-fabless-semiconductor-panel-don-t-pack-your-bags-just-yet.

[50] According to SEMI (the global industry association serving the manufacturing supply chain for the micro- and nano-electronics industries), Asia's share in worldwide wafer fabrication capacity is now 54 percent, and is expected to increase to more than 66 percent in 2015. See SEMI—*World Fab Watch 2014*, http://www.semi.org/en/Store/MarketInformation/fabdatabase/ctr_027237. Capacity comparisons are in equivalent 8-inch wafers.

[51] Semiconductor Industry Association, "Section 1: Industry Overview," http://www.semiconductors.org/clientuploads/Industry%20Statistics/2015%20Factbook/2015%20Factbook%20-%20Section%201%20-%2007212015.pdf. For instance, a recent survey of investments in chip fabrication equipment finds that China is the fastest-growing market, but this is primarily due to the ramp-up of the Samsung NAND Flash Memory fab in Xi'an, which is a $6.2 billion project. See *SEMI Forecasts Back-to-Back Years of Double-Digit Growth in Chip Equipment Spending*, July 7, 2014. http://www.semi.org/node/50436.

[52] US Department of Commerce 2015: p. 13.

[53] P. Clarke, "Apple Wins Place in Top 25 Chip Vendor Ranking," *Electronics 360*, April 22, 2015.

[54] W. Shih, *Semiconductor Manufacturing International Corporation (SMIC): 'Reverse* BOT,' HBS SMIC case study, 2009. http://www.hbs.edu/faculty/Pages/item.aspx?num=36733.

[55] *IC Insights*, "S. Korean and Taiwanese Companies Control 56% of Global 300mm Fab Capacity," 2014, http://www.icinsights.com/news/bulletins/S-Korean-And-Taiwanese-Companies-Control-56-Of-Global-300mm-Fab-Capacity/.

[56] *IC Insights*, "TI Strengthens Analog Market Share; Skyworks Gains from Apple's Favor," 2015, http://www.icinsights.com/news/bulletins/TI-Strengthens-Analog-Marketshare-Skyworks-Gains-From-Apples-Favor/

[57] PwC, 2014.

[58] 国务院关于印发"十二五"国家战略性新兴产业发展规划的通知 [The State Council Notification on the Long-term Development Plan for Strategic Emerging Industries during the 12th Five Year Plan], 国发〔2012〕28 号. July 7, 2012.

[59] As analyzed in D. Ernst and B. Naughton, *Global Technology Sourcing in China's Integrated Circuit Design Industry: A Conceptual Framework and Preliminary Findings*, East-West Center Working Papers, Economics Series, no. 131, 2012.

[60] See http://www.gov.cn/jrzg/2006-02/09/content_183787.htm and http://www.gov.cn/english/2006-02/09/content_184426.htm. For details, see chapter 2, in Ernst, D., 2011, *Indigenous Innovation and Globalization: The Challenge for China's Standardization* Strategy, UC Institute on Global Conflict and Cooperation; La Jolla, CA and East-West Center, Honolulu, HI. [Published in Chinese at the University of International Business and Economics Press in Beijing, 自主创新与全球化：中国标准化战略所面临的挑战]

[61] "We will strive to catch up with and overtake advanced countries in…new-generation mobile communications, integrated circuits, big data, advanced manufacturing…and to guide the development of emerging industries." Passage from PM Li Keqiang, *Government Work Report March 2014,* which specifically mentions "integrated circuits" in the context of "using innovation to support and lead economic structural improvement and upgrading."

[62] Tain-Jy Chen, 2015, "National Champions and Indigenous Innovation: The Case of the Chinese IC Design Industry," unpublished manuscript, Department of Economics, National Taiwan University.

[63] J.A. Schumpeter, *Capitalism, Socialism and Democracy* (New York: Harper & Row, 1942): 381.

[64] Chen 2015: 2.

[65] Chen, 2015: 27.

[66] Chen, 2015:.31.

[67] For the economics of global vertical specialization in IC design, see D. Ernst, "Complexity and Internationalization of Innovation: Why Is Chip Design Moving to Asia?" *International Journal of Innovation Management* 2005; and D. Ernst, "Limits to Modularity—Reflections on Recent Developments in Chip Design," *Industry and Innovation* 2005.

[68] D. Ernst, *A New Geography of Knowledge in the Electronics Industry? Asia's Role in Global Innovation Networks,* Policy Studies, no. 54 (Honolulu: East-West Center, 2009). That study provides a detailed analysis of the spread of global corporate networks of production and innovation in the electronics industry.

[69] Interview, June 22, 2012.

[70] D. Ernst and B. Naughton, 2012, *Global Technology Sourcing and China's Integrated Circuit Design Industry. A Conceptual Framework and Preliminary Research Findings, East-West Center Economics Working Paper # 131,* August 2012: 11–22

[71] Shanzhai (山寨) refers to Chinese imitation and pirated brands and goods, particularly for low-cost handsets. Literally "mountain village" or "mountain stronghold," the term refers to the mountain stockades of regional warlords or bandits, far away from official control.

[72] For details, see Part Three of this study, under section "Demand Pull for Mobile Devices as a Catalyst".

[73] Ernst and Naughton, 2012.

[74] Professor Wei Shaojun, as quoted in "China Fabless Semiconductor Panel: Don't Pack Your Bags Just Yet," http://community.cadence.com/cadence_blogs_8/b/ii/archive/2014/06/18/china-fabless-semiconductor-panel-don-t-pack-your-bags-just-yet. Dr. Wei is the dean of the Microelectronics Institute at Tsinghua University and president of the China IC Design Association, and China's representative in the World Semiconductor Council.

[75] The collision between two high-speed trains in Wenzhou on July 23, 2011, the third-deadliest HSR accident in history, provided an example of the high risks of top-down technology leapfrogging. (See S. Rabinovitch, "Crash Threatens China's High-Speed Ambitions," *Financial Times*, July 24, 2011.)

[76] An important insight of innovation theory is that, in general, catching up in high-tech industries like semiconductors takes time in order to develop the necessary skills, as well as the critically important intangible knowledge, and a great variety of complementary soft innovation capabilities that are necessary to develop a strong absorptive capacity. See, for instance, Kim, Linsu 1997, *Imitation to Innovation: The Dynamics of Korea's Technological Learning*, Harvard Business School Press, Boston, Mass; D. Ernst, 2002,"Global Production Networks and the Changing Geography of Innovation Systems: Implications for Developing Countries," *Economics of Innovation and New Technologies*, 11(6): 497-523; and D. Ernst., 2009, *A New Geography of Knowledge in the Electronics Industry? Asia's Role in Global Innovation Networks*, Policy Studies, no. 54, (Honolulu: East-West Center, 2009).

[77] For details, see "China's Fragmented Innovation System" in Part Three of the study.

[78] See, for instance, K. Walsh, *The Chinese Defense Innovation System*, presentation at IGCC Chinese Defense Industry Conference, June 30–July 1, 2011.

[79] Creating university-industry linkages has been the focus of much of Chinese attempts to reform its innovation system. More recently, attempts are under way to address the other disconnects, but so far with mixed results. See, for instance, chapter 2 in D. Ernst, *Indigenous Innovation and Globalization: The Challenge for China's Standardization Strategy* (La Jolla, CA: UC Institute on Global Conflict and Cooperation and Honolulu: East-West Center, 2011), http://www.EastWestCenter.org/pubs/3904. [Published in Chinese at the University of International Business and Economics Press in Beijing, 自主创新与全球化：中国标准化战略所面临的挑战].

[80] USITO, *"Guidelines to Promote National Integrated Circuit Industry Development"* (unauthorized translation of document published by the Ministry of Industry and Information Technology, the National Development and Reform Commission, the Ministry of Finance, and the Department of Science and Technology United States Information Technology Office, Beijing, June 24, 2014.

[81] Discussion during author's presentation at the US Semiconductor Industry Association (SIA), Washington, DC, September 18, 2014.

[82] Allen Lu, "Challenges and Opportunities for China in the Semiconductor Industry," SEMI Global Update, August 4, 2015: 1 and 6, www.semi.org.

[83] According to 2015 company reports.

[84] US-China Economic and Security Review Commission, *Monthly Analysis of the U.S.-China Trade Data*, "Sector Spotlight: China Aims to Boost Domestic Semiconductor Industry," August 5, 2015: 10–17.

[85] D. Simon, "The Microelectronics Industry Crosses a Critical Threshold," *The China Business Review* 28, no. 6 (2001): 8–20.

[86] *State Council Document 4 on Issuing Several Policies on Further Encouraging the Development of the Software and Integrated Circuit Industries* (January 28, 2011).

[87] Jones, H. 2014, "China needs a semiconductor industry", *China Daily,* October 7, http://usa.chinadaily.com.cn/epaper/2014-10/07/content_18701860.htm.

[88] See detailed discussion in Part Three of the study.

[89] A single nanometer (nm) is one million times smaller than a millimeter. Since integrated circuits, such as computer processors, contain microscopic components, nanometers are useful for measuring their size. In fact, different eras of processors are defined in nanometers, in which the number defines the distance between transistors and other components within the CPU. The smaller the number, the more transistors that can be placed within the same area, allowing for faster, more efficient processor designs. (See http://www.techterms.com/definition/nanometer.)

[90] See MIIT Vice-Minister Yang Xueshan, keynote speech at the Third Science and Technology Committee Annual Meeting in Beijing, August 19, 2014, http://www.miit.gov.cn/n11293472/n11293832/n11293907/n11368223/16113093.html. See also USITO, *China IC Industry Support Guidelines—Summary and Analysis*, September 1, 2014, Beijing.

[91] USITO, interview with Miao Wei, MIIT director of Department of Informatization, on the background, significance, and key points from the *Guidelines*, June 25, 2014: 3.

[92] Ibid.

[93] Wei Shaojun, quoted in Hsiao-Wen Wang, "China's Semiconductor Grab—TSMC, MediaTek in the Bull's Eye," *CommonWealth Magazine*, August 21, 2014, http://english.cw.com.tw/article.do?action=show&id=14830.

[94] US Department of Commerce, 2015: 13

[95] G. Dan Hutcheson, VLSI Research, quoted on 450mm wafer transition, in W. Izumiya, "450mm Wafer Transition Won't Happen Till 2020 at the Earliest," *The Semiconductor Industry News,* June 5, 2014, https://www.semiconportal.com/en/archive/news/news-by-sin/140605-sin-izumiya-may-vlsi.html.

[96] Gordon E. Moore, "Cramming More Components onto Integrated Circuits," *Electronics Magazine*, 1965: 4, http://www.cs.utexas.edu/~fussell/courses/cs352h/papers/moore.pdf.

[97] David M. Byrne, Stephen D. Oliner, Daniel E. Sichel, "Is the Information Technology Revolution Over?" (Washington, DC: Federal Reserve Board Finance and Economics Discussion Series/FEDS, March 2013), http://www.federalreserve.gov/pubs/feds/2013/201336/201336pap.pdf.

[98] Leo Mirani, "Chip-Makers Are Betting That Moore's Law Won't Matter in the Internet of Things," June 10, 2014, http://qz.com/218514/chip-makers-are-betting-that-moores-law-wont-matter-in-the-internet-of-things/.

[99] D. Ernst, *The Information Technology Agreement, Industrial Development and Innovation—India's and China's Diverse Experiences* (Geneva: The World Economic Forum and the International Center for Trade and Sustainable Development/ICTSD, 2014), http://e15initiative.org/wp-content/uploads/2014/11/E15_Innovation_Ernst_FINAL.pdf.

[100] USITO, 2014 interview with Miao Wei, page 3.

[101] The established view is that, in the words of a senior banker at HSBC, "…[t]he Chinese authorities don't like the 'big bang' approach. That's why they test something—and if it works, they do more of it." Justin Chan, co-head of markets for Asia-Pacific at HSBC, quoted in J. Noble, "Grand Global Ambitions for Currency Sow Domestic Risks," FT special report entitled *The Future of the Renminbi*, September 30, 2014: 2.

[102] USITO, 2014 interview with Miao Wei: page 4.

[103] USITO, 2014 interview with Miao Wei, page 4.

[104] For details, see Part Three of this study.

[105] "Yu Zhengsheng, from Wikipedia, the free encyclopedia." http://en.wikipedia.org/wiki/Yu_Zhengsheng.

[106] Yu started working as a technician in several radio factories in Hebei Province (1968–1975) before he joined the Research Institute for the Promotion and Application of Electronic Technology under the Fourth Ministry of Machine-Building Industry, where he served as a technician, engineer, and assistant chief engineer (1975– 1982). He was promoted to deputy director in 1982, after which he was transferred to the Ministry of Electronics Industry (MEI), where he served as head of the Department of Microcomputer Management, and later the MEI deputy director of planning (1982–84). Today, he is a strong promoter of China's IC industry's development. See http://www.brookings.edu/about/centers/china/top-future-leaders/yu_zhengsheng.

[107] If implemented, these policies are of quite some interest to current negotiations to expand the Information Technology Agreement (ITA). For instance, suppose China can use selective import tax exemptions, then what does

this imply for China's interest in ITA-2? Can import tax exemptions provide access to lower-cost critical inputs, so that import reductions via ITA-2 would be unnecessary?

[108] The following quotes are from USITO's unauthorized translation of the *Guidelines to Promote National Integrated Circuit Industry Development.*

[109] See https://www.qualcomm.com/news/releases/2015/02/09/qualcomm-and-chinas-national-development-and-reform-commission-reach. See also ChinaIPR, NDRC and Qualcomm Reach Resolution of Antimonopoly Law Complaint, http://chinaipr.com/2015/02/10/ndrc-and-qualcomm-reach-resolution-of-antimonopoly-law-complaint/.

[110] Quoted in P. Mozur, "Using Cash and Pressure, China Builds Its Chip Industry," *The New York Times*, October 26, 2014.

[111] Part Three of the study explores in some detail NDRC's treatment of Qualcomm and the surprisingly complex implications for China's innovation capacity in the mobile devices industry and the related semiconductors industry.

[112] See http://www.nytimes.com/2015/07/27/opinion/a-smart-deal-to-cut-tariffs-on-tech-products.html for a detailed analysis of China's approach to ITA-2 negotiations until Fall 2014. See also D. Ernst, *The Information Technology Agreement, Industrial Development and Innovation—India's and China's Diverse Experiences (*Geneva: The World Economic Forum and the International Center for Trade and Sustainable Development/ICTSD, 2014), http://e15initiative.org/wp-content/uploads/2014/11/E15_Innovation_Ernst_FINAL.pdf.

[113] See http://www.csia.net.cn/Article/ShowInfo.asp?InfoID=38790 and http://www.csia.net.cn/Article/ShowInfo.asp?InfoID=38789. (Both sources are in Chinese.)

[114] Leading groups have been extensively used since the early 1980s to foster the reform of China's science and technology system. See Tony Saich, "Reform of China's Science and Technology Organizational System," in *Science and Technology in Post-Mao China,* ed. D.F. Simon and M. Goldman (Harvard University: Council on East Asian Studies, 1989), 69–88.

[115] In 1982, the State Council funded a permanent leading group called the "Leading Group for Electronics, Computers, and Large-Scale Integrated Circuits." In 1984, the group's name was changed to the "State Council Leading Group for the Revitalization of Electronics [Industry]." The following year, the leading group published a document called "The Strategy for the Development of China's Electronics and Information Industries," which laid out strategies for the Seventh Five-Year Plan. For details, see D. Simon, *Technological Innovation in China: The Case of the Shanghai Semiconductor Industry* (Massachusetts: Ballinger Publishing, 1988).

[116] M. Pecht, *China's Electronics Industry: The Definitive Guide for Companies and Policy Makers with Interest in China* (Norwich, NY: William Andrew Publishing, 2006).

[117] Ministry of Industry and Information Technology, "Yan Xueshan Introduces the Essential Points of the Guidelines to Promote the National Integrated Circuit Industry," http://www.miit.gov.cn/n11293472/n11293832/n11293907/n11368223/16044279.html.

[118] Calculated from Semiconductor Industry Association, "Section 3: Capital and R&D Investment," slide 17, http://www.semiconductors.org/clientuploads/Industry%20Statistics/2015%20Factbook/2015%20Factbook%20-%20Section%203%20-%2007212015.pdf.

[119] Judy Lin and Steve Shin, "Taiwan IT Industries Facing Challenges from China Supply Chains, Says MOEA," *Digitimes*, July 21, 2015, http://digitimes.com/news/a20150721PD207.html.

[120] See SEMI, "China's Semiconductor Investment Plans Focus of SEMICON China 2015. Government Officials, Industry Leaders and Analysts Weigh Implications of Unprecedented Industry Investment," http://www.semi.org/node/54766.

[121] I am grateful to China-based contacts and former colleagues at UC Berkeley and in the Bay Area to trace the profiles of some of the persons involved. For guidance through the labyrinth of information on Chinese investment funds, I am grateful to Zhi Su, research associate for industry statistics and global policy, at the Semiconductor Industry Association.

[122] "Hua Capital Hires Bank of America for OmniVision Deal," *South China Morning Post*, September 19, 2014, http://www.scmp.com/business/companies/article/1595559/hua-capital-hires-bank-america-omnivision-deal.

[123] An informal inquiry, conducted by the author in Spring 2014 among fund managers in a leading global bank, showed that none of the interviewees knew CGP.

[124] See company web site, http://www.prosperityinvestment.hk/index.php?lang=tc.

[125] CGP's business philosophy is summed up in the following statement of its chairman: "Following the economic recovery of the United States of America, it started to reduce the scale of debt purchase in 2014, which affected the international fund flow. This may lead to the withdrawal of funds from various countries including China and Hong Kong, which in turn causes the instability of the stock market and the economy of these countries. However, this 'tight funding' situation may be an opportunity for the Group to identify potential investment at a lower investment cost. All in all, we will continue our investments in both China and Hong Kong with caution." Message from the chairman of CGP in the 2013 annual report, http://www.prosperityinvestment.hk/vtuploads/201404/LTN201404161316.pdf.

[126] As discussed below, Hua Capital Management Co., Ltd (HCM) is also managing China's acquisition of the US IC design company OmniVision.

[127] Chen Datong got his BS, MS, and PhD from Tsinghua University and worked as a post-doctoral research fellow at Stanford University. Dr. Chen has more than 20 years of investment and operations experience in the technology and semiconductor industries, and he owns 34 US and European patents. Prior to WestSummit, Datong was a venture partner at Northern Light Venture Capital, a leading technology VC fund, where he led investments in the semiconductor industry. Datong was the co-founder and CTO of Spreadtrum Communications, and hence has deep insider knowledge of that company. Prior to Spreadtrum, Dr. Chen was the co-founder and senior VP for OmniVision, again providing him with insider knowledge about the acquisition of that company, discussed below. Datong serves on the board of directors for two other important Chinese IC design companies, GigaDevice and VeriSilicon. Dr. Chen holds 34 global patents and has won the China Special Award for Inventor and Entrepreneur and named a Chinese Inventor in 2006. He is serving as counsel member of China Invention Association and China Semiconductor Association, and used to be the chairman of Tsinghua Entrepreneur and Executive Club (TEEC).

[128] USITO, *China IC Industry Support Guidelines—Summary and Analysis*, September 1, 2014: 6.

[129] The following information is taken from China Fortune-Tech Capital's website and from Tsinghua Unigroup's investor reports.

[130] For details on SMIC, see Part Three of this study.

[131] In light of these deep mutual interactions, it is somewhat difficult to accept at face value the following statement on the website of China Fortune-Tech Capital: "China Fortune-Tech will invest as financial investor, will not be investee's first shareholder and not control any of the investee. And China Fortune-Tech's investment will not impact SMIC's operation."

[132] The following analysis is based on interviews with observers and insiders of China's semiconductor industry. Where publicly available, key policy documents that shape China's new push in semiconductors have been consulted.

[133] USITO, 2014 interview with Miao Wei, page 3.

[134] GSMA, 2014, *Smartphone Forecasts and Assumptions, 2007–2020*, http://www.gsma.com/newsroom/press-release/smartphones-account-two-thirds-worlds-mobile-market-2020/.

[135] Data are from the Canalysis Country Market Tracker, October 2014, http://www.canalys.com/what-we-do/country-market-trackers. Examples include Chinese budget smartphones designed by Lenovo, Huawei, ZTE, and Xiaomi.

[136] I. Mansfield, "Chinese Phone Manufacturers Expected to Take Half the Market in 2015," *Cellular News*, March 10, 2014, cellular-news.com. The term original equipment manufacturer (OEM) is used here to refer to the company that acquires a product or component and reuses or incorporates it into a new product with its own brand name. For details, see D. Ernst, "Global Production Networks in East Asia's Electronics Industry and Upgrading Perspectives in Malaysia," in *Global Production Networking and Technological Change in East Asia*, eds. Shahid Yusuf, M. Anjum Altaf, and Kaoru Nabeshima (The World Bank and Oxford University Press, 2004).

[137] P. Goldstein, "Gartner, CCS Insight: Smartphone Growth in 2014 Will Be Fueled by Low-Cost Models," 2014, http://www.fiercewireless.com/story/gartner-ccs-insight-smartphone-growth-2014-will-be-fueled-low-cost-models/2014-10-15.

[138] Canalysis, "Xiaomi Becomes China's Top Smart Phone Vendor," August, 4, 2014, http://www.canalys.com/newsroom/xiaomi-becomes-china%E2%80%99s-top-smart-phone-vendor.

[139] PwC 2014, quoting data from the China Semiconductor Industry Association (CSIA), MIIT, and Gartner, the US consulting firm.

[140] For an analysis of China's TD-SCDMA standard, see chapter 5 in D. Ernst, *Indigenous Innovation and Globalization: The Challenge for China's Standardization Strategy* (La Jolla, CA: UC Institute on Global Conflict and Cooperation and Honolulu: East-West Center, 2011). [Published in Chinese at the University of International Business and Economics Press in Beijing, 自主创新与全球化：中国标准化战略所面临的挑战]

[141] Note, however, that according to Canalysis, "…Xiaomi has risen from being a niche player to become the leading smart phone vendor in the world's largest market, overtaking Samsung in volume terms in Q2. Xiaomi took a 14% share in China, on the back of 240% year-on-year growth." (See http://www.canalys.com/newsroom/xiaomi-becomes-china%E2%80%99s-top-smart-phone-vendor.) These data need to be taken with a grain of salt—the often quite substantial differences in market share estimates of different consulting firms indicate the fluidity and unpredictability of the rapidly evolving smartphone market.

[142] This is now beginning to change. When Xiaomi introduced its new smartphone software MIUI 7 (which is based on Google's Android operating system) on August 20, 2015, media reports were highly critical, highlighting a "deep lack of innovation." Clover, C., 2015, "Xiaomi underwhelms in saturated market," *Financial Times*, August 21:14.

[143] J.P.V. Sampere, "Xiaomi, Not Apple, Is Changing the Smartphone Industry," *Harvard Business Review*, October 14, 2014, https://hbr.org/2014/10/xiaomi-not-apple-is-changing-the-smartphone-industry/.

[144] As predicted in A. Stevenson-Yang and K. DeWoskin, "China Destroys the IP Paradigm," *Far Eastern Economic Review* 168, no. 3 (2005): 9–18. That article focuses on the impact of reverse engineering of foreign technology, forced technology transfer, and IP theft, but does not address explicitly strategic patenting.

[145] See https://qualcommventures.com/team-member/james-shen/.

[146] For details, see D. Ernst, *Global Strategic Patenting and Innovation—Policy and Research Implications*, East-West Center Working Papers, Innovation and Economic Growth Series, no. 2, 2015, http://www.eastwestcenter.org/system/tdf/private/iegwp002.pdf?file=1&type=node&id=34977.

[147] Courtesy of statistics data base of the Chinese Patent Office SIPO, http://english.sipo.gov.cn/.

[148] See https://www.qualcomm.com/news/releases/2015/02/09/qualcomm-and-chinas-national-development-and-reform-commission-reach. See also "NDRC and Qualcomm Reach Resolution of Antimonopoly Law Complaint," http://chinaipr.com/2015/02/10/ndrc-and-qualcomm-reach-resolution-of-antimonopoly-law-complaint/.

[149] In December 2014, Ericsson successfully litigated Xiaomi in India, a critical market for Xiaomi's planned overseas expansion. And rumors are ripe that Huawei and ZTE are preparing litigation in China, and that Apple sooner or later will follow suit.

[150] A recent study, commissioned by the Government Accountability Office (GAO) for the America Invents Act, defines patent monetization companies as "those entities whose primary focus is deriving income from licensing and litigation, as opposed to making products." See S. Jeruss, R. Feldman, and J. Walker, *The American Invents Act 500: Effects of Patent Monetization Entities on US Litigation*, Duke Law and Technology Review 11, no. 2 (2012–2013): 361. http://scholarship.law.duke.edu/cgi/viewcontent.cgi?article=1239&context=dltr.

[151] P. Waldmeier, "Great Leap Backwards at Li-Ning," *Financial Times*, January 24, 2015, page 10.

[152] D. Sambandaraksa, "Living with the Xiaomi MI3," *Telecom Asia*, September 10, 2014, http://www.telecomasia.net/blog/content/living-xiaomimi3?section=INSIGHT&utm_source=silverpop&utm_medium=newsletter&utm_content=&utm_campaign=telecomasia.

[153] *Forward Concepts Wireless Newsletter*, August 14, 2014, page 1.

[154] A. Chen and L. Lin, "China 4G Smartphone Demand Fails to Surge: CoolPad, Lenovo, Xiaomi Unlikely to Achieve 2014 Targets," *DigiTimes*, October 1, 2014.

[155] Data are from the IDC Worldwide Quarterly Mobile Phone Tracker, August 17, 2014, http://www.idc.com/search/other/perform_.do?sortBy=RELEVANCY&_xpn=false&cg=5_1321&srchIn=ALLRESEARCH&src=&athrT=10&lang=English&cmpT=10&page=1&hitsPerPage=50.

[156] E. Anderson et al., *Measuring the U.S.-China Innovation Gap: Initial Findings of the UCSD-Tsinghua Innovation Metrics Survey Project*, STI Policy Brief no. 14, December 2013, http://www-igcc.ucsd.edu/assets/001/505418.pdf.

[157] On August 4, 2014, TSMC reported that it has received 28nm chip orders from more than 10 China-based IC design houses and design service providers (C. Chao and S. Shen, "China-based IC Design Houses Ramping 28nm Chip Orders at TSMC," *DigiTimes*, August 4, 2014). The companies mentioned in the announcement comprise all of China's leading IC design firms, i.e., HiSilicon, Spreadtrum, Rockchip, Allwinner, RDA, and Datang.

[158] Ed Pausa, PwC, email to the author, August 18, 2014.

[159] M. Li, "Chinese Fabless Industry to Outgrow Semiconductor Sector by Significant Margin," *The Wall Street Transcript*, May 26, 2014.

[160] China Market Research reports, 2015, Global and China Wafer Foundry Industry Report, 2013-2014, http://www.chinamarketresearchreports.com/114904.html.

[161] Wei Shaojun, quoted in Hsiao-Wen Wang, "China's Semiconductor Grab—TSMC, MediaTek in the Bull's Eye," *CommonWealth Magazine*, August 21, 2014, http://english.cw.com.tw/article.do?action=show&id=14830.

[162] *SMIC Investor Fact Sheet*, 2014, http://www.smics.com/eng/investors/ir_sheet.php.

[163] Tzu-Yin Chiu, CEO of Semiconductor Manufacturing International Corp. (SMIC), quoted in Y. Yoshida, "Will SMIC Narrow Tech Gap," *EETimes*, March 27, 2014.

[164] For a detailed discussion of more recent developments, see below section 5. A new interest in strategic partnerships and mergers and acquisitions.

[165] An EEPROM, or electrically erasable programmable read only memory, like a regular ROM chip, uses a grid and electrical impulses in order to create binary data. However, the difference between ROM chips and EEPROM chips is that EEPROM chips can be reprogrammed without removing them from the computer, contrary to basic ROM chips which can only be programmed one time, https://www.futureelectronics.com/en/memory/eeprom.aspx.

[166] Microelectromechanical systems, or MEMS, are defined as miniaturized mechanical and electromechanical elements (i.e., devices and structures) that are made using the techniques of microfabrication. The critical physical dimensions of MEMS devices can vary from well below one micron on the lower end of the dimensional spectrum, all the way to several millimeters. Likewise, the types of MEMS devices can vary from relatively simple structures having no moving elements, to extremely complex electromechanical systems with multiple moving elements under the control of integrated microelectronics. The one main criterion of MEMS is that there are at least some elements having some sort of mechanical functionality, whether or not these elements can move. For more information, see https://www.mems-exchange.org/MEMS/what-is.html.

[167] This cooperation focuses on manufacturing MEMS-based oscillators, designed to allow direct post-processing of high-quality MEMS layers on top of Silicon Labs's RF/mixed-signal CMOS technology. Another joint venture with a US company, Toppan Photomasks Inc., in Round Rock, Texas, seeks to manufacture on-chip color filters and micro-lenses for CMOS image sensors. And SMIC's new R&D and manufacturing center seeks to develop proprietary MEMS process technology, as well as manufacturing capabilities for silicon-based sensors and trailing-node wafer process technologies.

[168] Author's interview, July 14, 2014.

[169] J. Yoshida, "China Erects First 12in IC Manufacturing Supply Chain," *EETimes*, August 11, 2014.

[170] "Wafer bumping" is replacing wire bonding as the interconnection of choice for a growing number of components. The broad term "wafer bumping" is defined as the process by which solder, in the form of bumps or balls, is applied to the device at the wafer level. The use of wafer bumping is driven either by performance, form factor, or array interconnect requirements. The ability to properly design the device for bumping will have direct bearing on manufacturability, reliability, and cost-savings from wafer fabrication through component assembly. (See D.S. Patterson, "The Back-end Process: Step 7—Solder Bumping Step by Step," *Solid State Technology* 44, issue 7 (July 1, 2001), http://electroiq.com/blog/2001/07/the-back-end-process-step-7-solder-bumping-step-by-step/.

[171] According to Wikipedia, wafer testing is a step performed during semiconductor device fabrication. During this step, performed before a wafer is sent to die preparation, all individual integrated circuits that are present on the wafer are tested for functional defects by applying special test patterns to them. The wafer testing is performed by a piece of test equipment called a wafer prober. The process of wafer testing can be referred to in several ways: Wafer Sort (WS), Wafer Final Test (WFT), Electronic Die Sort (EDS), and Circuit Probe (CP) are probably the most common.

[172] micrometer = μm.

[173] QST holds worldwide and exclusive license of Honeywell's AMR magnetic sensor technology. In addition, QST holds patents in a number of CMOS integrated multi-axis motion sensors.

[174] *IC Insights*, "Samsung Invests Big to Maintain Leadership, Support New Markets," *IC Insights Research Bulletin*, October 15, 2014.

[175] "Foundry Ranking by Capacity 2013–2014," http://anysilicon.com/foundry-ranking-capacity-2013-2014/.

[176] See the 2014 McClean Report, http://www.icinsights.com/news/bulletins/Top-13-Foundries-Account-For-91-Of-Total-Foundry-Sales-In-2013/. With annual sales of about $5.4 billion, Samsung would be ahead of the 2013 sales of Global Foundries, the current Number 2 in the IC Foundry ranking.

[177] "IBM Fabs for Sale—the Semiconductor Shockwave," *Electronics Weekly*, February 10, 2014, http://www.electronicsweekly.com/news/business/viewpoints/ibm-fabs-sale-semiconductor-shock-2014-02/#sthash.p1E0hyzx.dpuf.

[178] R. Merritt, "IBM Strikes Historic Fab Deal with Global Foundries," *EETAsia,* October 21, 2014.

[179] R. Waters, "IBM's Troubles with Cloud Send Profits Tumbling," *FT*, October 21, 2014, front page. According to industry insiders, IBM management was under quite some pressure from Warren Buffett, IBM's biggest shareholder, whose stake has been drastically reduced by IBM losses.

[180] See the website of Intel's Custom Foundry Group, http://www.intel.com/content/www/us/en/jobs/campaigns/foundry-jobs.html.

[181] This agreement culminated on June 1, 2015, in Intel's proposed acquisition of Altera.

[182] For details of Intel's deals with Rockchip and Spreadtrum, see Section 5 below.

[183] *IC Insights*, "Leading-Edge IC Foundry Market Forecast to Increase 72% in 2014," *IC Insights Research Bulletin*, September 25, 2014.

[184] The process of merging Spreadtrum and RDA was actually quite complex. On December 23, 2013, Tsinghua Unigroup announced the US$1.7 billion acquisition of Spreadtrum, "as contemplated by the previously announced agreement and plan of merger, dated as of July 12, 2013 (the 'Merger Agreement'), between Tsinghua Unigroup and Spreadtrum." "Tsinghua Unigroup Completes Acquisition of Spreadtrum for US$31.00 per ADS, http://www.prnewswire.com/news-releases/tsinghua-unigroup-completes-acquisition-of-spreadtrum-for-us3100-per-ads-237053401.html. And on July 19, 2014, Tsinghua Unigroup announced the "approximately US$907 million merger of RDA Microelectronics with an affiliate of Tsinghua Unigroup (the 'Merger') as contemplated by the previously announced agreement and plan of merger, dated November 11, 2013, and amended on December 20, 2013 (the 'Merger Agreement'), between Tsinghua Unigroup and RDA." Tsinghua Unigroup Closes US$907 Million Acquisition of RDA Microelectronics for US$18.50 Per ADS, http://archive.is/xVa1h#selection-911.0-915.1.

Most likely, this complicated process was necessary to get the pre-clearance from the NDRC, the responsible Chinese government agency.

[185] D. Bushell-Embling, "Qualcomm Bringing LTE-A to Low-cost Phones," *Telecom Asia*, September 11, 2014.

[186] Anonymous Chinese industry observer, quoted in J. Yoshida, "Battle of Spreadtrum/RDA Merger," *EETimes*, March 21, 2014.

[187] Email to the author by Will Strauss, president of Forward Concepts (Tempe, Arizona), August 22, 2014.

[188] For details, see Ernst and Naughton, 2012: chapter 4.

[189] Spreadtrums's SC883XG platform integrates current best-practice 3G mobile standards from the 3GPP international standard development organization that draws on Europe's GSM standard and includes China's TD-SCDMA standard. 3GPP stands for The 3rd Generation Partnership Project.

[190] Mr. Vincent Tai is RDA's co-founder and has been chairman of RDA's board of directors and chief executive officer since the company's inception in 2004.

[191] *IC Insights Research Bulletin*, "Tsunami of M&A Deals Underway in the Semiconductor Industry in 2015," http://www.icinsights.com/news/bulletins/Tsunami-Of-MA-Deals-Underway-In-The-Semiconductor-Industry-In-2015/.

[192] "NXP and Freescale Shareholders Meetings Approve Merger," http://www.nxp.com/news/press-releases/2015/07/nxp-and-freescale-shareholders-meetings-approve-merger.html.

[193] Avago Technologies to Acquire Broadcom for $37 Billion, http://investors.avagotech.com/phoenix.zhtml?c=203541&p=irol-newsArticle&ID=2053937. Headquartered in Singapore, Avago Technologies is a designer, developer, and supplier of analog, digital, mixed signal, and optoelectronics components and subsystems, drawing on broad technology portfolio from erstwhile technology leaders like HP, AT&T, and LSI Logic. Broadcomm, a US IC design company, headquartered in Irvine, CA, with a focus on wireless and broadband communication devices.

[194] Headquartered in San Jose, CA, Altera is a US IC design company with a strong position in Programmable Logic Devices, reconfigurable complex digital circuits.

[195] "Intel's $16.7 Billion Altera Deal Is Fueled by Data Centers," http://www.bloomberg.com/news/articles/2015-06-01/intel-buys-altera-for-16-7-billion-as-chip-deals-accelerate.

[196] During the first half of 2015, a wave of mergers and acquisitions has hit the semiconductor industry, as chipmakers try to gain scale, cut operating expenses, and grow their cross-selling opportunities by consolidating. Important deals include: Qualcomm's acquisition of Cambridge Silicon Radio (CSR); Infineon's acquisition of International Rectifier; Cirrus Logic's purchase of Wolfson Electronics; the merger between RF Micro Devices and TriQuint Semiconductor; Avago's purchase of LSI Corp; and Microchip's acquisition of Bluetooth chipmaker ISSC.

[197] *IC Insights Research Bulletin*, "Tsunami of M&A Deals Underway in the Semiconductor Industry in 2015," http://www.icinsights.com/news/bulletins/Tsunami-Of-MA-Deals-Underway-In-The-Semiconductor-Industry-In-2015/.

[198] Very little information on these efforts is in the public domain. This study relies on informal background information provided by industry observers who require anonymity.

[199] While Qualcomm refuses to provide details, the deal most likely is for Qualcomm's Snapdragon 210 processor, a low-cost chip for 4G LTE budget smartphones that features multimode 3G/LTE and LTE Dual SIM support. (See D. Bushell-Embling, "Qualcomm Bringing LTE-A to Low-cost Phones," *Telecom Asia*, September 11, 2014.)

[200] J. Yoshida, "Is SMIC-Qualcomm 28nm Deal One-Sided?" *EETimes,* July 7, 2014.

[201] J. Lien and S. Shen, "UMC Lands 28nm LTE Chip Orders from Qualcomm, Say Sources," *DigiTimes*, October 14, 2014. According to industry sources, these chips are to be used for the production of iPhone 6 smartphones, which seems to indicate that UMC is expected to continue to receive more follow-up orders from Qualcomm.

[202] Zvi Or-Bach has more than 20 years of experience in the IC design industry, and holds over 100 issued patents, primarily in the field of 3D integrated circuits and semi-custom chip architectures. For more information, see http://www.monolithic3d.com/zvi-bio.html.

[203] Z. Or-Bach, comments on J. Yoshida, "China's SMIC-Qualcomm 28-nm Deal: Why Now?" *EETimes,* July 3, 2014. On the underlying technological transformations, see also Z. Or-Bach, "Qualcomm Calls for Monolithic 3D IC," *EETimes*, June 17, 2014.

[204] According to GSA, "…[a]s geometries continue to shrink and 2D scaling becomes increasingly difficult, 3D-IC packaging becomes a natural alternative to continued advances in ever smaller footprints; it is the convergence of performance, power, and functionality. Many of the benefits of 3D-IC packaging, such as increasing complexity while simultaneously improving performance, reducing power consumption, and decreasing footprints are proven and readily understood. Other benefits such as improving time-to-market, lowering risk, and lowering cost will be conquered as 3D-IC packaging becomes a commercially viable solution across many application domains." See http://www.gsaglobal.org/working-groups/3d-ic-packaging/.

[205] Quoted in Z. Or-Bach, "Qualcomm Calls for Monolithic 3D IC," *EETimes*, June 17, 2014.

[206] See http://www.smics.com/attachment/201407181552332_en.pdf.

[207] Z. Or-Bach, comments on J. Yoshida, "China's SMIC-Qualcomm 28-nm Deal: Why Now?" *EETimes,* July 3, 2014.

[208] IMEC research institute in Louvain, Belgium, is a world-leading semiconductor research institute. Its global innovation network includes research centers in the Netherlands, Taiwan, USA, China, India, and Japan. For more information, see http://www2.imec.be/be_en/about-imec.html.

[209] As reported in Allen Lu, "Challenges and Opportunities for China in the Semiconductor Industry," SEMI Global Update, August 4, 2015, www.semi.org.

[210] Lu, 2015.

[211] ASE (= Advanced Semiconductor Engineering, Inc, Taiwan) is the world's largest provider of independent semiconductor manufacturing services in assembly and test.

[212] Texas Instruments acquires UTAC facility in Chengdu, China, http://investor.ti.com/releasedetail.cfm?ReleaseID=815042. Headquartered in Singapore, UTAC is a leading provider of test and assembly services for a wide range of semiconductor devices.

[213] Siliconware Technology (Suzhou) Limited engages in manufacturing and processing of module assembly and testing, flash memory card and related products.

[214] See discussion earlier in the study.

[215] Lu, 2015

[216] Founded in 2001, Fuzhou Rockchip Electronics Co. develops system-on chip solutions for Android tablet, Android TV box (Smart TV), e-book, and WIFI/Bluetooth audio solutions. The company has combined its video/audio and Android experience to produce semiconductor (IC) solutions for leading global contract manufacturers and brand name companies. Rockchip is headquartered in Fuzhou, where most design and development is taking place, and has three additional branches in Beijing, Shanghai, and Shenzhen, focusing mostly on software and marketing. See www.rock-chips.com.

[217] C. Chao and A. Hwang, "International Smartphone Chip Vendors Enhance Development of Tablet Chips," *Digitimes*, October 21, 2014.

[218] M. Chen and J. Tsai, "Intel Aims to Ship 25 Million Tablet Processors in the Second Half of 2014," *Digitimes*, August 26, 2014.

[219] E. Lin, "Intel, Rockchip Look to Expand the x86 Presence in Tablet AP Market," *Digitimes*, September 22, 2014.

[220] "Intel and Tsinghua Unigroup Collaborate to Accelerate Development and Adoption of Intel-based Mobile Devices," http://newsroom.intel.com/community/intel_newsroom/blog/2014/09/25/intel-and-tsinghua-unigroup-collaborate-to-accelerate-development-and-adoption-of-intel-based-mobile-devices.

[221] G. Shih and N. Randewich, "Intel to Invest Up to $1.5 Billion in Two Chinese Mobile Chipmakers," September 26, 2014, http://www.reuters.com/article/2014/09/26/us-spreadtrum-m-a-intel-idUSKCN0HK29R20140926.

[222] For the economics of system-on-chip design, see D. Ernst, "Complexity and Internationalization of Innovation: Why is Chip Design Moving to Asia?" *International Journal of Innovation Management*, March 2005, special issue in honor Keith Pavitt.

[223] J. Yoshida, "4 Reasons for Intel's $1.5 Billion Bet in China," *EETimes*, September 26, 2014.

[224] "Omnivision Announces Receipt of Non-Binding Acquisition Proposal," http://www.reuters.com/finance/stocks/OVTI.O/key-developments/article/3050441.

[225] "Hua Capital Hires Bank of America for OmniVision Deal," *South China Morning Post*, September 19, 2014, http://www.scmp.com/business/companies/article/1595559/hua-capital-hires-bank-america-omnivision-deal.

[226] "OmniVision To Be Acquired By Hua Capital Management, CITIC Capital And GoldStone Investment For $29.75 Per Share In Cash," *PR Newswire*, April 30, 2015, http://www.prnewswire.com/news-releases/omnivision-to-be-acquired-by-hua-capital-management-citic-capital-and-goldstone-investment-for-2975-per-share-in-cash-300075052.html.

[227] The Committee on Foreign Investment in the United States (CFIUS) is an interagency committee of the United States government that reviews the national security implications of foreign investments in US companies or operations. For details, see http://www.treasury.gov/resource-center/international/Pages/Committee-on-Foreign-Investment-in-US.aspx.

[228] USITO email to the author, dated October 23, 2014.

[229] "Chinese State Owned Firm Launches Takeover of US Chip Giant Micron," http://www.wsj.com/articles/state-owned-chinese-chip-maker-tsinghua-unigroup-makes-23-billion-bid-for-micron-1436833492.

[230] I am grateful to Ed Pausa at PwC for sharing his analysis of the Thomson Reuter database.

[231] There were 64 other transactions where the acquirer was from a different nation, including the US (16), Hong Kong (10), Singapore (5), Japan (4), and others.

[232] "China Govt to Bid for Broadcom Cellular Unit—Report," *Telecompaper News*, June 25, 2014, http://www.telecompaper.com/news/china-govt-to-bid-for-broadcom-cellular-unit-report--1021572.

[233] See discussion earlier in this study.

[234] I am grateful to Falan Yinug of the US Semiconductor Industry Association (SIA), for sharing these data.

[235] Other industries, like car and aircraft, are also large consumers of semiconductors. Hence, the role of semiconductors for China's total goods exports is significantly higher.

[236] The following arguments are based on written comments from SIA emailed to the author, dated September 26, 2014.

[237] SIA email to the author, dated September 26, 2014.

[238] K. Lieberthal, *Managing the China Challenge: How to Achieve Corporate Success in the People's Republic* (Washington, DC: Brookings Institution Press, 2011), 21.

[239] Lieberthal, 2011, 26.

[240] This section draws on D. Ernst, *China's Fragmented Innovation System*, presented at the University of California Institute on Global Conflict and Cooperation/Department of Defense DARPA symposium entitled "What Is DARPA in Chinese? The Nature and Prospects for Radical Defense R&D and Innovation in China," June 29, 2011, University of California at San Diego.

[241] Alan Wm. Wolff, "China's Indigenous Innovation Policy," testimony before the US China Economic and Security Review Commission Hearing on China's Intellectual Property Rights and Indigenous Innovation Policy, Washington, DC, May 4, 2011.

[242] This is true for China's definition of products that contribute to indigenous innovation, the revision of government procurement regulations, and new regulations for patents included in standards. For a detailed analysis, see Chapter 4 in D. Ernst, *Indigenous Innovation and Globalization: The Challenge for China's Standardization Strategy* (La Jolla, CA: UC Institute on Global Conflict and Cooperation and Honolulu: East-West Center, 2011). [Published in Chinese at the University of International Business and Economics Press in Beijing, 自主创新与全球化：中国标准化战略所面临的挑战.]

[243] S. Kennedy, "Indigenous Innovation: Not as Scary as It Sounds," *China Economic Quarterly*, September 2010, 19–20.

[244] The following draws on chapter two in D. Ernst, *Indigenous Innovation and Globalization: The Challenge for China's Standardization Strategy*, 2011. See also D. Ernst and S. Martin, *The Common Criteria for Information Technology Security Evaluation: Implications for China's Policy on Information Security Standards*, East-West Center Working Paper, Economics Series no. 108, January 2010.

[245] S.L. Shirk, *China: Fragile Superpower—How China's Internal Politics Could Derail Its Peaceful Rise* (Oxford, UK: Oxford University Press, 2007).

[246] A *backdoor* is a secret or undocumented means of getting into a computer system. Many programs have backdoors placed by the programmer to allow them to gain access to troubleshoot or change the program. Some backdoors are placed by hackers once they gain access to allow themselves an easier way in next time, or in case their original entrance is discovered. A *loophole* is a weakness or exception that allows a system, such as a law or security, to be circumvented or otherwise avoided. Loopholes are searched for and used strategically in a variety of circumstances, including taxes, elections, politics, the criminal justice system, or in breaches of security. The *Trojan horse*, in the context of computing and software, describes a class of computer threats (malware) that appears to perform a desirable function, but in fact performs undisclosed malicious functions that allow unauthorized access to the host machine, giving hackers the ability to save their files on the user's computer or even watch the user's screen and control the computer. Trojan viruses can be easily and unwillingly downloaded.

[247] A study on the damage to America's ICT industry caused by NSA global surveillance practices concludes: "The recent revelations about the extent to which the National Security Agency (NSA) and other U.S. law enforcement and national security agencies have used provisions in the Foreign Intelligence Surveillance Act (FISA) and USA PATRIOT Act to obtain electronic data from third-parties will likely have an immediate and lasting impact on the competitiveness of the U.S. cloud computing industry if foreign customers decide the risks of storing data with a U.S. company outweigh the benefits." (From D. Castro, *How Much Will PRISM Cost the U.S. Cloud Computing Industry?* Information Technology and Innovation Foundation publication, 2013, http://www2.itif.org/2013-cloud-computing-costs.pdf.

[248] Quoted from USITO, *USITO Summary and Analysis—China IC Industry Support Measures*, September 1, 2014, e5.

[249] After all, security concerns as a tactic to mobilize support for public and private investment in R&D have been used in other countries before, the United States included.

[250] In contrast to multilateral WTO agreements, where all WTO members are party to the agreement, a megaregional agreement implies that WTO member countries have a choice to agree to new rules on a voluntary basis. For details, D. Ernst, and M. Plummer, *Mega-Regionalism: New Challenges for Trade and Innovation*, paper prepared in 2015 for an Agenda-Setting Workshop, co-funded by the National Science Foundation and the East-West Center, Honolulu, January 20–21, 2016, http://www.eastwestcenter.org/events/mega-regionalism-new-challenges-trade-and-innovation.

[251] ITA went into effect in April 1997 with 29 World Trade Organization (WTO) member countries. Unlike other plurilateral agreements, ITA provides "most favored nation" (MFN) treatment to all WTO members, even if those countries have not joined the agreement. Today, ITA has 78 WTO members—36 are non-Organisation for Economic Co-operation and Development (OECD) member countries, and 35 are developing countries. They include significant players in the electronics industry (China, Taiwan, Malaysia, Thailand, and Vietnam), as well as other countries—such as India, Egypt, Indonesia, Philippines, and Turkey—that have the potential to become players. In its current form, ITA provides zero tariffs for 217 electronics products. The main product groups covered are computers, semiconductors, semiconductor manufacturing and test equipment, telecommunications equipment, software, and scientific instruments. For details, see WTO, *15 Years of the Information Technology Agreement, Trade, Innovation and Global Production Networks* (Geneva: World Trade Organization, 2012).

[252] From a global welfare perspective, trade expansion could reinforce the diffusion of innovation, as argued in J. Curtis, "Trade and Innovation: Challenges and Policy Options," background paper for Expert Group 6 meeting, ICTSD, Geneva, June 6–7, 2013.

[253] For an optimistic scenario, see, for instance, S.J. Ezell, *Boosting Exports, Jobs and Economic Growth by Expanding the ITA* (Washington, DC: Information Technology and Innovation Foundation/ITIF, March 2012), 8–9. For a comparative analysis of India's and China's experiences with ITA, see D. Ernst, *The Information Technology*

Agreement, Industrial Development and Innovation—India's and China's Diverse Experiences (Geneva: The World Economic Forum and the International Center for Trade and Sustainable Development/ICTSD, 2014), http://e15initiative.org/wp-content/uploads/2014/11/E15_Innovation_Ernst_FINAL.pdf.

[254] As quoted in S. Donnan, "Negotiators Nervously Eye China's Resistance in IT Trade Talks," *Financial Times*, November 19, 2013, http://www.ft.com/intl/cms/s/0/9456096e-5112-11e3-b499-00144feabdc0.html#axzz2srbBkrjM.

[255] "Taiwan Caves, Says It Will Accept ITA Deal without Flat-Panel Displays," *China Trade Extra*, July 27, 2015.

[256] Email to the author from Peter Petri, January 28, 2014.

[257] For detailed analysis, see D. Ernst, "Complexity and Internationalisation of Innovation: Why Is Chip Design Moving to Asia?" *International Journal of Innovation Management* 9, no. 1 (March 2005): 47–73. See also D. Ernst, *A New Geography of Knowledge in the Electronics Industry? Asia's Role in Global Innovation Networks*, Policy Studies, no. 54 (Honolulu: East-West Center, 2009).

[258] B. Kogut and U. Zander, "Knowledge of the Firm and the Evolutionary-Theory of the Multinational Corporation," *Journal of International Business Studies* 24, no. 4 (1993): 625–645.

[259] For an analysis of the increasing complexity and diversity of global innovation networks, see D. Ernst, "Trade and Innovation in Global Networks—Regional Policy Implications," in *Can Policy Follow the Dynamics of Global Innovation Platforms?* ed., Jos Leijten (Delft, Netherlands: The International Innovation Policy Network of the Six Countries Programme, 2014).

[260] A. Grove, *Only the Paranoid Survive* (New York: Doubleday, 1996).

[261] P. Marsh, "Marvel of the World Brings Both Benefit and Risk," *Financial Times,* June 11, 2010, page 7. For a detailed case study of the multilayered global production networks in Asia's ICT industry, see D. Ernst, "Global Production Networks in East Asia's Electronics Industry and Upgrading Perspectives in Malaysia," in *Global Production Networking and Technological Change in East Asia,* eds., Shahid Yusuf, M. Anjum Altaf, and Kaoru Nabeshima, The World Bank and Oxford University Press, 2004.

[262] D. Ernst, *A New Geography of Knowledge in the Electronics Industry? Asia's Role in Global Innovation Networks*, Policy Studies, no. 54 (Honolulu: East-West Center, 2009).

[263] The company has pursued a two-pronged strategy (see Ernst, D. and B. Naughton, "China's Emerging Industrial Economy-Insights from the IT Industry," 2007): It is building a variety of linkages and alliances with leading global industry players and universities, while concurrently establishing its own global innovation network of more than 25 R&D centers worldwide. Huawei's own GIN now includes, in addition to at least eight R&D centers in China, five major overseas R&D centers in the United States, and at least ten R&D centers in Europe (See chapter two of D. Ernst, 2014, "Trade and Innovation in Global Networks – Regional Policy Implications", chapter 3 in Jos Leijten, ed., *Can Policy Follow the Dynamics of Global Innovation Platforms?* The International Innovation Policy Network of the Six Countries Programme, Delft. The choice of these locations reflects Huawei's objective to be close to major global centers of excellence and to learn from incumbent industry leaders: Plano, Texas, is one of the leading US telecom clusters initially centered on Motorola; Kista, Stockholm, plays the same role for Ericsson and, to some degree, Nokia; and the link to British Telecom was Huawei's entry ticket into the exclusive club of leading global telecom operators.

[264] L.S. Jordan and K. Koinis, *Flexible Implementation: A Key to Asia's Transformation*, Policy Studies, no. 70 (Honolulu: East-West Center, 2014).

[265] D. Ernst, "Trade and Innovation in Global Networks—Regional Policy Implications," in *Can Policy Follow the Dynamics of Global Innovation Platforms?* ed., Jos Leijten (Delft, Netherlands: The International Innovation Policy Network of the Six Countries Programme, 2014).

[266] OECD, *Innovation-driven Growth in Regions: The Role of Smart Specialisation—Preliminary Version* (Paris: OECD, 2013). For the underlying concept of "smart specialization," see D. Foray, *Smart Specialisation: Opportunities and Challenges for Regional Innovation Policy Opportunities and Challenges for Regional Innovation Policy* (Routledge, 2014).

Acknowledgments

The study owes much to detailed comments by Chen Tain-Jy (National Taiwan University, Taipei); William Bonvillian (MIT Office, Washington, DC); Stephan Haggard(School of Global Policy and Strategy, University of California at San Diego); Wang Ping (China National Institute for Standardization/CNIS, Beijing); Ambassador Alan Wm. Wolff (Chairman, National Foreign Trade Council/NFTC, Washington, DC); and Mark Wu (Harvard Law School, Cambridge, MA). The author greatly benefited from discussions with Jeffrey Alexander (SRI, Washington, DC); An Baisheng (World Economics Research Institute/Ministry of Foreign Trade and Commerce); Rob Atkinson (The Information Technology Innovation Foundation/ITIF, Washington, DC); Suzanne Berger (Production in the Innovation Economy Project/PIE, MIT, Cambridge, MA); David M. Byrne (Federal Reserve Board, Washington, DC); Adam Century (US Information Technology Office/USITO, Beijing); Chen Ling (Tsinghua University, Beijing); Peter Cowhey (School of International Relations and Pacific Studies, University of California at San Diego); David F. Cowhig (US State Department); Michael Ding (IGRS Information Industry Association, Beijing); Ambassador Charles Freeman (Projects International, Inc., Washington, DC); Gao Xudong (Department of Innovation, Entrepreneurship and Strategy, Tsinghua University, Beijing); Jimmy Goodrich (US Semiconductor Industry Association/SIA, Washington, DC); Gary Herrigel (University of Chicago); Derek L. Hill (National Science Foundation, Washington, DC); Kent Hughes (Wilson Center, Washington, DC); David Isaacs (US Semiconductor Industry Association/SIA, Washington, DC); Cynthia Johnson (Texas Instruments, Washington, DC); Simon Johnson (MIT Sloan School of Management, Cambridge, MA); Luke S. Jordan (Johannesburg, South Africa); Scott Kennedy (Freeman Chair in China Studies, Center for Strategic and International Studies, Washington, DC); Paul Lengermann (Federal Reserve Board, Washington, DC); Liu Xielin (School of Management, University of Chinese Academy of Sciences, Beijing); Mu Rong Ping (Institute of Policy and Management, Chinese Academy of Sciences, Beijing); Barry Naughton (School of International Relations and Pacific Studies, University of California at San Diego); Timothy Neely (US State Department); Marcus Noland (Peterson Institute for International Economics and East-West Center); Clements Ed Pausa (Pricewaterhouse Coopers LLP); Peter Petri (Brandeis University and East-West Center); Michael G. Plummer (Johns Hopkins University SIAS, Bologna, and East-West Center); Pedro Roffe (International Centre for Trade and Sustainable Development/ICTSD, Geneva); Stephen Schlaikjer (CENTRA Technology, Washington, DC); Willy Shih (Harvard Business School, Cambridge, MA); Stephanie S. Shipp (Virginia Bioinformatics Institute at Virginia Tech, Science and Technology Policy Institute); Song Mingshun, (School of Economics and Management, China Jiling University, Hangzhou); Ed Steinfeld (Watson Institute, Brown University, Providence, RI); Zhi Su (US Semiconductor Industry Association/SIA, Washington, DC); Richard P. Suttmeier (Center for Asian and Pacific Studies, University of Oregon); Charles Wessner (National Academy of Sciences, Washington, DC); Yang Xia (Legend Capital, Beijing); Falan Yinug (US Semiconductor Industry Association/SIA, Washington, DC); Shahid Yusuf (The Growth

Dialogue, George Washington University, Washington, DC); Zhang Gang (OECD, Paris); Zhang Lei (Shanghai University of International Business and Economics, Shanghai); Zhang Yan (IBM China, Beijing); and Zhiyong, Alan Fan (Huawei, Beijing). As always, however, any errors and mistakes are my responsibility.

At the East-West Center, I am grateful to Charles E. Morrison (president), and Nancy D. Lewis (director of research) for supporting research on trade and innovation across the Asia Pacific, including a new multi-year series of agenda-setting workshops on *Mega-Regionalism: New Challenges for Trade and Innovation*; and to Elisa Johnston, Carol Wong, and Sharon Shimabukuro for the fast and effective publication of this study.

About the Author

Dieter Ernst, an East-West Center senior fellow, is an authority on global production networks and the internationalization of research and development in high-tech industries, with a focus on standards and intellectual property rights. Ernst is the co-founder, together with Michael G. Plummer (Johns Hopkins University SIAS, Bologna) of the agenda-setting workshop series *Mega-Regionalism—New Challenges for Trade and Innovation*, funded by the National Science Foundation, on the impact of trade agreements on trade and innovation in Asia. Ernst's research examines corporate innovation strategies and innovation policies in the United States and in China, India, and other emerging economies. The author has served as a member of the United States National Academies' Committee on Global Approaches to Advanced Computing; senior advisor to the Organisation for Economic Co-operation and Development (OECD), Paris; research director of the Berkeley Roundtable on the International Economy at the University of California at Berkeley; professor of international business at the Copenhagen Business School; and scientific advisor to governments, private companies, and international institutions.

Dieter Ernst's public talks include: Keynote address to international conference *Solid-State Lightning (SSL) China 2015*, Shenzhen Exhibition Center, November 2–4, 2015; "Standardization, International Trade, and Government Policies," IEEE-SIIT 9th International Conference on Standardization and Innovation in Information Technology, San Jose, California, October 6–7, 2015; keynote address: "Innovation in Global Networks—The Challenge for Technical Standards and Related Policies," Department of Commerce–NIST workshop; "Supply Chain Operations, Strategy, and Infrastructure Development in a Global Economy," Georgetown University, May 18–19, 2015; "Global Strategic Patenting and Innovation—Policy and Research Implications," keynote address at the Six Countries Program conference "40 Years of Innovation Policy: What's Next?" House of Research, Vienna, March 24–25, 2015 (available as East-West Center Working Paper, Innovation and Economic Growth Series, no. 2, February 2005).

His publications include *Standards, Innovation, and Latecomer Economic Development: Conceptual Issues and Policy Challenges* (2014); *Trade and Innovation in Global Networks—Regional Policy Implications* (2014); *The Information Technology Agreement, Industrial Development and Innovation—India's and China's Diverse Experiences* (2014); *Upgrading India's Electronics Industry—Regulatory Reform and Industrial Policy* (2014); *Industrial Upgrading through Low-Cost and Fast Innovation—Taiwan's Experience* (2013); *America's Voluntary Standards System: A "Best Practice" Model for Asian Innovation Policies?* (2013); Entry on "Production and Innovation Networks, Global" (*Encyclopedia of Global Studies, 2012); Indigenous Innovation and Globalization: The Challenge for China's Standardization Strategy* (2011; also published in Chinese); *China's Innovation Policy Is a Wake-Up Call for America* (2011); *A New Geography of Knowledge in the Electronics Industry? Asia's Role in Global Innovation Networks* (2009); *Can Chinese IT Firms Develop Innovative Capabilities within Global Knowledge Networks?* (2008); *China's Emerging Industrial Economy: Insights from the IT Industry* (with

Barry Naughton, 2007); *Innovation Offshoring: Asia's Emerging Role in Global Innovation Networks* (2006); *Complexity and Internationalization of Innovation: Why Is Chip Design Moving to Asia?* (2005); *Limits to Modularity—Reflections on Recent Developments in Chip Design* (2005); *Global Production Networks, Knowledge Diffusion and Local Capability Formation* (with Kim Linsu, 2002); *International Production Networks in Asia: Rivalry or Riches?* (2000); and *Technological Capabilities and Export Success: Lessons from East Asia* (1998).

www.ingramcontent.com/pod-product-compliance
Lightning Source LLC
Chambersburg PA
CBHW051338200326

41519CB00026B/7474